Anatomy of a Food Addiction: The Brain Chemistry of Overeating, by Anne Katherine, M.A.

Behind the 8-Ball: A Guide for Families of Gamblers, by Linda Berman, M.S.W., and Mary-Ellen Siegel, M.S.W.

Believing in Myself: Daily Meditations for Healing and Building Self-Esteem, by Earnie Larsen and Carol Hegarty

Blues Ain't Nothing But a Good Soul Feeling Bad: Daily Steps to Spiritual Growth, by Sheldon Kopp with Bonnie B. Hesse

Codependents' Guide to the Twelve Steps, by Melody Beattie

Family Intervention by Frank L. Picard, M.S.

Freedom from Food: The Secret Lives of Dieters and Compulsive Eaters, by Elizabeth Hampshire

From Love That Hurts to Love That's Real: A Recovery Workbook, by Sylvia Ogden Peterson

Growing Through the Pain: The Incest Survivor's Companion, by Catherine Bronson

Growing Up Gay in a Dysfunctional Family: A Guide for Gay Men Reclaiming Their Lives, by Rik Isensee

Help for Helpers: Daily Meditations for Those Who Care

Hooked on Exercise: How to Understand and Manage Exercise Addiction, by Rebecca Prussin, M.D., Philip Harvey, Ph.D., and Theresa Foy DiGeronimo

Repressed Memories: A Journey to Recovery from Sexual Abuse, by Renee Fredrickson, Ph.D.

Soul Survivors: A New Beginning for Adults Abused as Children, by J. Patrick Gannon, Ph.D.

Understanding the Twelve Steps: An Interpretation and Guide for Recovering People, by Terence T. Gorski

Repressed Memories

A JOURNEY TO RECOVERY FROM SEXUAL ABUSE

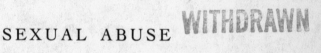

RENEE FREDRICKSON, PH.D.

A Fireside/Parkside Book

Published by Simon and Schuster

New York   London   Toronto   Sydney   Tokyo   Singapore

FIRESIDE/PARKSIDE

Rockefeller Center
1230 Avenue of the Americas
New York, New York 10020

FIRESIDE and colophon are registered trademarks
of Simon & Schuster Inc.

FIRESIDE/PARKSIDE is a trademark of Simon & Schuster Inc.

PARKSIDE is a trademark of Parkside Medical Services Corporation.

Library of Congress Cataloging-in-Publication Data
is available.

7   9   10   8

ISBN: 0-671-76716-X

Designed by Quinn Hall
Manufactured in the United States of America

Parkside Medical Services Corporation is a full-service
provider of treatment for alcoholism, other drug addiction,
eating disorders, and psychiatric illness.

Parkside Medical Services Corporation
205 West Touhy Avenue
Park Ridge, IL 60058
1-800-PARKSIDE

A CAUTION TO READERS

The information in this book is intended for educational purposes only. It is not intended to replace diagnosis and treatment by competent professionals. The contents are designed to be used as an adjunct to a rational and responsible sexual abuse recovery program guided by a mental health professional or physician. The author and publisher are in no way liable for the use or misuse of the information in this book.

Memory recovery work should be done *only* under the care of a competent mental health professional, particularly if the reader has any one or more of the following conditions:

- suicidal thoughts
- self-injury or mutilating behaviors

- a history of psychotic episodes
- any difficulty distinguishing between reality and fantasy
- multiple personality disorder
- flashbacks in which it is impossible to distinguish between memory and reality

ACKNOWLEDGMENTS

So many people gave of themselves to make this book possible that I see myself as a voice for all my contributors rather than a solitary author. My dear family, Jeremy, Joseph, and Selena, not only gave their love but also gave up substantial portions of my time and attention. Jeremy especially offered support, invaluable advice, and long days studying beside me so I would not flee from the demands of my word processor. My lifelong friends and colleagues, Jacquie Trudeau and Cheryl Beardslee, profoundly shaped the ideas in this book. I am deeply grateful for their unshakable faith in this and every other project I have undertaken. Carol Phelps, my partner in Dallas, could always see what I could not and offered her wisdom and insight generously.

Pat Collins stood ready at the telephone or in the staff room, always willing to help me clarify a concept or find an elusive word or phrase. Warren Shaffer listened patiently as I struggled with logic and form, fine-tuning the book with his feedback. Dr. Peg Thompson gave unstinting support throughout the process, as well as generously sharing her ideas and allowing them to be presented in this book.

Kip Leonard was always there for me, believing in the book and me whenever I faltered, while Carla Bowyer kept my life, my office, and my sense of humor intact. Diana Kowalczyk offered support in the office, and Phoebe Johnson offered her support to me and my family. My own family-of-origin also gave me their love and encouragement. Sheila Curry provided expert editing. Finally, Sarah Jane Freyman, my agent, gave me more encouragement and help than any first-time author could ask for, and I will always be grateful for her help.

The greatest contribution however, came from the survivors of abuse who shared their stories of suffering and recovery with me. A few of them are presented in the case examples in the book, with names and facts in their stories changed to conceal their identities. Many more are part of the very fabric of the book. They are the clients who allowed me to walk with them on their journey to recovery, forgiving my mistakes and enlightening my understanding of sexual abuse, repressed memories, and recovery. They deserve my heartfelt thanks, and this book is dedicated to them for their courage, honesty, and patience.

CONTENTS

INTRODUCTION

Eighteen years ago I began my career as a psychother-
apist as an intern at an outpatient therapy clinic. My
first client was a woman who told me that her father
had raped her from the time she was four years old until
she was eighteen. In all my graduate and undergraduate
work as a psychology major, no one had made a single
reference to the existence of sexual abuse. Needless to
say, I was at sea about how to help this courageous
young woman. The appalling lack of available resources
for treating sexual abuse influenced me to specialize in
this area.

Once my practice was established, I received
hundreds of referrals of sexually abused children, as well
as adults. I was saddened to discover that many of these
child victims were as young as one or two years old.
Working with these little ones sparked my interest in re-

pressed memories. Some of the babies seemed to remember vaguely what happened to them, while others acted out their abuse without apparent conscious memories.

I soon realized that many of the adults I was working with had been abused at an early age and that the lessons I was learning about the feelings and needs of very young children applied to adult survivors as well. The children I was seeing were younger versions of what my adult clients were twenty or thirty years earlier. Seeing these children enhanced my work with adult survivors who were abused at an early age, and I got my first glimmer of awareness about repressed memories.

My colleagues and I established a clinic in St. Paul, Minnesota, and ten years later a friend and I opened a second clinic in Dallas, Texas. I began lecturing in the United States and in Canada, and I became a consultant to the U.S. Army on child abuse. My professional experience widened to incorporate the thousands of sexual abuse cases to which I was exposed.

I first became interested in the healing of repressed memories several years ago when I was doing marathon therapy workshops in Dallas. It seemed as if client after client was suddenly having memories of being sexually abused by their father, mother, grandfather, or neighbor. I was suspicious at first. I thought that this must be some form of contagious hysteria. As I became increasingly convinced of the reality of the clients' memories, I then wondered if the phenomenon were some strange anomaly of the Southern patriarchal system. I certainly had not encountered as many repressed memories of abuse in my home state of Minnesota.

As my awareness grew, I found that there were as many people with buried memories of abuse in the Midwest as in the South. Like sexual abuse in general, the more you know about what to look for with repressed memories, the more you find. Just as clients' stories of incest were met with skepticism and controversy, I found many people were skeptical about clients' repressed memories of abuse.

My foray into the psychological literature revealed almost nothing on repressed memories. I did find a few case examples in the lesser-known journals, mostly involving art therapy or hypnotherapy. And I was angered to discover in the psychoanalytic literature case after case of children and adults struggling to tell Freudian analysts about abuse, only to have the person's story turned into a fantasy by the analyst about "penis envy," "castration anxiety," or "sexual impulses toward the parent." I was forced to rely on my own observations and the clinical experiences of my colleagues to learn about repressed memories.

I must admit I still thought of buried memories of abuse as something of a rarity. Nonetheless, I decided to give a lecture as an impetus for me to articulate more clearly the work I was doing on memory repression. My St. Paul office staff mailed out 25 flyers, and I expected perhaps 10 or so people to come to the talk. Over 120 people showed up. I was astounded.

Later I repeated the lecture for my office in Dallas. Over 140 people came this time. I also taped this lecture to offer for sale, and again I was surprised to find people ordering this tape, through word of mouth, from all over the country.

Finally, I realized the size of the problem. Millions of people have blocked out frightening episodes of abuse, years of their life, or their entire childhood. They want desperately to find out what happened to them, and they need the tools to do so.

I began to listen to my clients with focused attention to the possibility of buried memories. Strange dreams, half-finished sentences, strong reactions to abuse issues, and imagery that persistently bothered my clients began to take on new meaning. People in recovery from abuse, ever sensitive to the hope that someone might listen and believe them, opened up to share their fears and secretly held beliefs about what happened to them in childhood. From my clients' stories, imagery, and dreams, I began to put together a system with which to facilitate the recovery of repressed memories of abuse.

This book is a compilation of all that I learned. I sincerely hope those of you who have repressed memories haunting your life will find it a useful guide. I realize now that there are so many of you who need this information. I also hope you find some comfort in knowing that there are countless others who wondered why the pain they felt seemed so much greater than the abuse they remembered.

GUIDING YOUR OWN RECOVERY

Everything you need to heal is inside yourself. You only need support and encouragement to listen to yourself—to your thoughts, feelings, imagery, and inner spiritual urgings. A book, like a therapist or a group, can only guide you, helping you to say out loud what you dared not say even to yourself. Please remember this in your reading about repressed memories.

Unfortunately, recovering memories of abuse is a painful process. Some of you may find that going through the process brings up feelings, images, and impulses that frighten and overwhelm you. If this happens, slow down, ask for help, and even stop the process, if necessary. The whole of who you are now is more important than your past and is too precious to damage. There is no disgrace in deciding not to look at your past when you are not feeling strong enough. If you do not have a therapist, you should seek one out to help you through this time.

Believing yourself is empowering, while letting others help and counsel you fosters trust and intimacy. I advise you to use this book with the skilled guidance of a caring professional. Do not be ashamed of getting help. Remember the saying "None of us is as smart as all of us."

I will focus primarily on repressed memories of sexual abuse. I do not mean to diminish the struggle of those of you working with repressed memories of physical or emotional abuse. Using sexual abuse as a model for repressed memories gives a sharper focus for descriptions and case examples. Those of you who believe you were not sexually abused can apply nearly all the information on sexual abuse memory repression to your memories of physical and emotional abuse amnesia. Be alert, however, for the possibility that you were sexually abused but have denied and repressed that abuse.

Chapter One introduces you to the concept of repressed memories of abuse and how they impact your life. Chapter Two offers you information about warning signs that may indicate the presence of repressed memories, which will be useful in giving you a chance to see if you show some of the classic indicators of memory repression. Chapters Three and Four present a clear model for how children develop this kind of amnesia and in what kind of family setting. All four of these chapters may challenge your denial.

Denial is the art of pretending not to know what you know. It is not defeated by logic, insight, information, or confrontation, although all of these play a part in its demise. Denial is overcome only by patient growth in the opposite direction. It eases over time, returning periodically to taunt you with the possibility of your own foolishness. In reading this book, whenever you find yourself worrying—"What if I'm wrong?"—try to always ask yourself the opposite question—"What if I'm right?"

The remainder of the book focuses on how to facilitate recovery of repressed memories. Some of these are suggestions or techniques that are new and, hopefully, will be helpful to you. You may have other strategies that work well for you, or you may find your memories returning spontaneously. In any case, persevere in whatever helps you. Avoid falling into the trap that says you must do it "right." Do what works best for you.

Many of you, plagued by the crippling disbelief that is the hallmark of repressed memories, will want to rush to Chapter Nine to find out if you are fabricating terrible tales of abuse to extort sympathy. Although you may find this chapter useful, it will not fully resolve this struggle for you. The battle to believe is too tied to your denial and the myths in your family system for any ten or twenty pages of print to settle. You will be too busy thinking up ways that you are an exception to the rules. I advise you to slow down, read the preceding chapters, and carefully observe all your reactions to the book.

The last chapter gives suggestions to complete your healing process, but I want to stress that getting your memories back is the most healing process of all. Healing begins the moment you recover your first memory and continues throughout the time it takes you to give shape and substance to your hidden past. Do not confuse healing with the absence of pain, for healing wounds, whether physical or emotional, always hurt. I can only assure you that the hurt will pass, and the pain will lessen.

At the end of each chapter is a section called "Empowering Yourself." This part of the book is designed to help you apply what you have learned from each chapter to your own repressed memories. The exercises and questions are not a step-by-step guide to recovery, for each person has a wondrous complexity and uniqueness that makes it impossible to create a single recovery road map that fits everyone. Instead, use this section as a guide and a stimulus in your recovery.

I hope all of you read this book with a journal nearby

and a support network of a therapist, group, Twelve-Step organization, loved ones, and friends who are available to talk over what you learn about your memories. Journal writing and support are keystones to recovery. We write the unthinkable and say the unspeakable with these tools, and repressed memories are just that to us—unthinkable and unspeakable.

Recovery is about healing and hope. Read the chapters on healing with an awareness that your recovery is a promise you made to yourself. There are many forces in the universe that will help you keep that promise. You may have pain, but you do not have a tragic flaw. You may feel hopeless, but that is only a feeling, not a prediction. Renewal is a gift available to all.

CHAPTER ONE

A DAWNING REALITY

Sarah was walking in the bright summer sunshine with her husband of six months. She was relaxed, enjoying her new husband, the beautiful day, and the brisk, invigorating exercise. She thought, "I have never been so happy." Suddenly, she was gripped by a wave of pure terror. She could not breathe, and her whole body began to tremble. Paralyzed by fear, she was convinced she was dying. Her husband desperately tried to persuade her that she was having a panic attack, not a premonition of her own death.

Sarah is beginning a journey into the world of repressed memories. She was sexually abused as a young child, and, because she was so young and so frightened when it happened, she buried all memory of that abuse. Now the time bomb that is abuse is ready to explode, and she is about to face what happened to her. She will experience frightening sensations, bizarre flashbacks, and terrifying nightmares. Her view of her family and childhood will change. At times she will be torn with doubts about her emerging reality.

At the end of her trip through her memories, she will emerge more serene than she had ever thought possible, as she finally accepts the childhood trauma that shaped her adult life. Self-defeating behaviors and troublesome feelings will cease to plague her when she comes to an understanding of their origins. The pain she has always carried and thought was a necessary component of the human condition will be lessened. Her journey is one of healing.

WHAT ARE REPRESSED MEMORIES?

You do not remember everything that happens to you. Not every moment of your daily life is preserved in your conscious memory, nor is every holiday or birthday recalled in detail. Memory repression is a useful and necessary tool that unburdens your mind, leaving you free to focus your conscious energy on the here and now.

The traumatic and the trivial are the two kinds of information your mind represses. Other than passing pop quizzes in school, you have no need to remember inconsequential information. Your mind consigns most unnecessary information to your memory banks.

Trauma is any shock, wound, or bodily injury that may be either remembered or repressed, depending on your needs, your age, and the nature of the trauma. Some of your childhood traumas may be remembered with incredible clarity, while others are so frightening or incomprehensible that your conscious mind buries the memory in your unconscious.

If the trauma that is repressed is an accidental injury, major illness, or any shock that is witnessed by others, it becomes part of your oral history. Your family tells the story at holidays and reunions of the time Claire fell down the stairs, Jeff broke his leg, or Angie had to be in the hospital for five weeks. The trauma may not be remembered, but Claire knows why she is too scared to walk downstairs without holding the handrail, Jeff knows why his leg often aches in rainy weather, and Angie is aware of why she is so frightened of hospitals.

Abuse and Repressed Memories

Abuse is a particular form of trauma done by one human being to another. Abuse, simply defined, is a trauma inflicted deliberately, wrongly, and unjustly to harm another human being. It is the only kind of trauma that your family will not talk to you about.

If you have repressed memories of childhood trauma, the memories are undoubtedly about abuse. Your family will tell you about your two-year-old temper tantrums or the terrible fall you had off your bike, but no one will mention that Grandpa seemed to maneuver to spend a lot of time alone with you when you were a little girl. Abuse is all too often a family secret, with the perpetrator and the family honor protected by a strict no-talk rule.

Repressed memories are not only likely to be about abuse; they are also more likely to be about sexual abuse than physical or emotional abuse. Although all forms of abuse can result in repressed memories, sexual abuse is particularly susceptible to memory repression. Memory repression thrives in shame, secrecy, and shock. The shame and degradation experienced during a sexual assault is profound, especially for children who have no concept of what is happening to them or why. Sexual abuse is so bizarre and horrible that the frightened child feels compelled to bury the event deep inside his or her mind.

Sexual abuse is also a secret crime, one that usually has no witness. Shame and secrecy keep a child from talking to siblings about the abuse, even if all the children in a family are being sexually abused. In contrast, if a child is physically or emotionally abused, the abuse is likely to occur in front of the other children in the family, at least some of the time. The physical and emotional abuse becomes part of the family's explicit history. Sexual abuse does not.

Learning from Repressed Memories

Repressed memories are pieces of your past that have become a mystery. They stalk your unconscious and hamper your life with their aftermath. They will tell you a story if you know how to listen to them, and the story will help you make sense of your life and your pain. As the story unfolds, you wonder if your mind is playing a trick on you, causing you to make up a strange, sad, and sometimes horrifying tale of abuse.

Your mind has played a trick on you, but it is a trick to help you rather than hurt you. When you were abused you were too young and too fragile to retain the memory, or you may have undergone torment too appalling to handle it in any other way. You needed your strength for play, for learning, for seeking and holding on to whatever love you could find in your world. So your wonderful, powerful mind hid some or all of the abuse from you until you were strong enough to face it.

Your repressed memories were held in storage not only for your readiness but also for society's readiness to deal with them. There has been an evolution of consciousness in our culture, resulting in a renewed awareness and ability to humanely respond to abuse. More and more of you are remembering your childhood suffering as you sense the increased capacity for validation and healing from the world around you.

YOUR JOURNEY

All journeys require a route, risk, and bravery. This book will give you some possible routes, but you will supply the bravery and risk-taking. Deciding to take control and actively search for your hidden past means facing painful feelings and challenging your family's reality. You may not want to embark on such a journey, but you may find you need to in order to have recovery and serenity in your life.

The journey to retrieve your repressed memories is one of discovery and healing. It is an internal journey in which you must piece together mind and body clues to find out what you have forgotten. You will struggle at first to believe what you are remembering, but your healing will take place as you recover your memories.

Some of you are aware that you have repressed memories. You need no convincing of the importance of this arduous journey. You desperately want information to improve your ability to recall further memories of abusive incidents. You do not need encouragement to continue to remember, for your memories are returning on their own timetable. You do need assistance on your journey and, above all, validation that your journey does indeed have an end.

Audrey suspected she had repressed memories throughout most of her adolescence and adulthood. She described her experience as having a dark cloud hanging over her memory of her childhood. "I knew something terrible had happened to me. There was this awful sense that I had forgotten something really hideous and really important."

When she heard of a therapist who was experienced in working with repressed memories, Audrey made an appointment with her immediately. With minimal guidance from the therapist, her memories came flooding back. Images of sexual abuse by both her mother and her father began surfacing, and she had no trouble labeling the images as memories and believing them. The relief she felt in doing so was enormous. "I've got my history back," she said. "I know who I really am now."

For others of you, uncovering your repressed memories is a survival issue. The damage from the abuse is so profound that your life and physical well-being are in grave danger. You may be suicidal, tempted to sexually abuse others, or inflicting deliberate, crippling injury on your body. These impulses and behaviors are telling you a story about your history and will not subside until the past is uncovered.

Mike had repressed all memory of his mother's sexual and physical abuse. He had tried to kill himself with carbon monoxide, but his roommate found him in time. When he began therapy, he was contemplating suicide again, and his arms were covered with self-inflicted cigarette burn scars. He did not expect to live.

Through the course of his therapy, he recovered memories of his mother's sexual assaults. She would force him to have oral sex with her and then beat him, screaming that he was evil and deserved to die. Working through this abuse enabled Mike to claim his life as his own. "You don't have to be Freud to figure out why I wanted to die," he said. "Now I figure I've suffered enough for my mother. I don't want to die for her."

Many more of you are reluctant to undertake the arduous journey of discovering your repressed memories. You suspect you have been abused but wonder if you shouldn't let sleeping dogs lie. Why even try to bring back memories of something so painful you had to forget it in the first place? "I really don't need to know," you might say. "My life is hard enough as it is."

In reality, your life is harder than it need be because you were abused. Dealing with that abuse will enable you to achieve more serenity in your life. My associates and I have a maxim that says the amount of fear you feel about confronting abuse is directly proportional to the impact it is having on your life right now. The greater your fear, the more the abuse is marring your current life.

Carolyn was someone who was reluctant to embark on a journey into her past. She did not know she had been abused, but her life was fraught with problems that she could not seem to resolve. She was a compulsive overeater, but rationalized that being overweight is a common malady in America. She could not establish a permanent relationship with a man. "I attract alcoholics like flies," she complained. She threw herself into her job, but it seemed to take most of her energy. When she developed stress-related backaches and headaches, her physician suggested she see a therapist.

Carolyn resisted probing into her family-of-origin in therapy. "My parents did the best they could," she asserted. "Besides, I have enough problems in my life. Why bother looking for more?" Slowly and painfully the story of her father's alcoholism and her competitive, cold relationship with her mother emerged.

Then the nightmares started. Night after night, Carolyn dreamt of a young child crying endlessly. Her efforts to save the child were always futile, and she would awaken trembling and frightened. Doing dream work helped her to understand the cry for help from the sobbing child.

The dreams shifted to explicit scenes of Carolyn being sexually abused. She also began seeing flashes of pictures of a small girl being orally and vaginally penetrated by a slim, dark-haired man. The image in her dream fit the physical description of her father, but she recoiled in horror at the possibility that the dream figure assaulting her might be her father.

"Not my dad!" she cried. "It couldn't be him. It just doesn't fit with who he is. I always felt sorry for him because he's so pathetic."

Gradually, Carolyn came to believe that she had been sexually abused and that her father was her abuser. Her anger and grief were enormous. For months she suffered emotionally, physically, and spiritually. She had crying jags, eating binges, suicidal feelings, and bouts of depression. She also caught every flu or virus making the rounds and had a severe flare-up of a pelvic infection.

As she dealt with her memories and feelings, she decided to confront her parents with her memories. They denied them vehemently, calling her crazy and demented. The only support she got from them for her reality was her mother saying, "Your father always did have a high sex drive, even around you." Her mother then refused to explain what she meant by that comment.

Carolyn persisted. She told her sisters and brother what she remembered. She talked to friends and her support group as she struggled with her feelings. She worked on her dreams and images, and, through them, realized that her father had abused her many, many times.

She faced all this trauma with courage and grace, and her efforts paid off. The nightmares faded. Her health improved dramatically, her depression lifted, and she had long stretches of serenity in her life for the first time. She began to use her therapy hour to talk about her current life issues instead of her memories. After dating several men who could not give her what she wanted, she started a relationship with a kind, supportive man. With his encouragement she joined Overeaters Anonymous and experienced relief from her compulsive eating.

"I never felt like my problems were connected to my past, and, to be honest, they still don't seem related," Carolyn said. "But I'm sure it's not a coincidence that, after I dealt with my repressed memories, I finally had the energy and stamina to make some headway on my personal problems."

THE IMPACT OF REPRESSED MEMORIES

Mental health professionals and the public are aware that sexual abuse causes lifelong damage. The after-effects are varied and pervasive. A deep sense of sexual shame, depression, anxiety, worthlessness, guilt, and difficulties with careers and relationships are some of the well-documented consequences of childhood sexual abuse.

The Missing Connection

Unfortunately, you are not likely to associate the current problems you are having with your emotions, relationships, or career with past abuse. During an abusive incident victims dissociate, separating or distancing themselves from the abuse. You numb yourself in order to survive.

Hurt, shame, and anger are the emotional result of abuse. Because you dissociate from your feelings during the abuse, you do not experience them until the dissociation wanes. The connection is lost between the abuse and the feelings the abuse caused. When the feelings inevitably surface, you no longer realize what the feelings are about because of the extended length of time between the abuse and the emergence of the feelings.

Without knowledge of the source of these emotions, the negative feelings are often directed inward, resulting in self-hate, depression, and self-destructive behaviors. They may also be directed outward, culminating in destructive behaviors or involvement in abusive relationships. Wherever they are directed, they cause problems in your life—problems you do not associate with abuse.

If you remember the abuse, however, you have a chance to trace the connections between your current life struggles and your abuse history. Problems that at first seemed overwhelming or inexplicable begin to make sense when you look at how you were mistreated in the past. Armed with this information, you can debrief your abusive experiences and set about creating a new, healthier life for yourself.

What if you do not remember the abuse? You are left with all the pain, all the negative feelings, and all the self-defeating behaviors without a clue to their origin. You blame yourself for problems that are the result of your abuse, never suspecting that what you are struggling with has its origins in your childhood.

Repressed memories affect your quality of life. Just like remembered sexual abuse, repressed memories of abuse are associated with such problems as failed relationships, depression, anxiety, addictions, career struggles, and eating disorders. The list is as varied as the human spirit. If you have buried memories of abuse, the problem you feel the most hopeless and shameful about is undoubtedly bound up with the abuse you suffered.

Rewards

Deciding to search out the hidden secrets in your past will be as rewarding as it is painful. Not only will you have the opportunity to finally address the damage from the abuse itself but you will also be able to free yourself from the burden of carrying repressed trauma memories. Burying memories and keeping them buried takes mental energy. When you bring those memories to the conscious level, your mind and body will no longer have to struggle to suppress such a heavy load.

Some of your symptoms that are the result of unresolved abuse issues will simply fade as you confront your returning memories. Other difficulties will require more of your energy for resolution, but dealing with the abuse will give you that energy. Your recovery process will free up the necessary creative capabilities to tackle the stubborn, seemingly hopeless problems in your life.

Sexual abuse also damages your self-esteem. Survivors are left feeling dirty, shameful, and ugly. You will come to realize that those feelings were not about who you are but what was done to you. Retrieving your memories allows you to place those feelings where they belong—on your perpetrators.

When you retrieve your repressed memories, you get the tremendous reward of knowing your own history. Needing to know who you are and where you came from is a powerful drive in people. Survivors with repressed memories are left with a disjointed sense of their own history and suffer from a sense of incompleteness. Even if you can make reasonable deductions about what happened to you, you feel haunted and overwhelmed without the specific memories. As painful as they may be to retrieve, you will finally know what the missing pieces are in your childhood.

Once you know, you can grieve. You were deeply hurt by the silence and betrayal of the abuse, and you are sad about all that happened and all that might have been. This unresolved grief is as inaccessible as the memories are. When you recover the memories, you have a chance to finish the grieving. You will always have a place of sadness in you for the abused child that was you, but it will no longer be an agonizing, untouched wound. Grieving hurts, but when you are finished you can move on.

Facing what you do not remember about your past is a challenging odyssey. Yes, it will hurt for a while, but you are probably already suffering from the damage from the abuse. Uncovering repressed memories will give you the chance to end that suffering.

EMPOWERING YOURSELF

Write down or share with a friend how you feel about working with your repressed memories. What do you want to gain from it? What do you want to be different in you life? What are you most afraid of? How do you think your family-of-origin will react?

Gather your support network around you. Tell your friends, therapist, and any support groups you are in about your decision to delve into your memories. Ask them for their support and involvement, and be as specific as possible about what you want. Offer your support to those who reveal that they are also looking at their repressed memories. This is not only generosity on your part but helping someone else will allow you to learn more about your own process.

If you suspect or know that you have repressed memories of abuse, how do you think the abuse has affected your life? How do you think your sense of self was damaged? Picture your recovery in your own mind, and see yourself resolving some or all of these problems as you recover. How does that change your view of yourself?

Let yourself know what the most hopeless or shameful problem in your life is. Try saying to yourself three or four times a day for one week, "I believe this problem is about my repressed memories of abuse." After a week, write down or talk over with a friend how you see the problem now. Speculate on how it may relate to how you were abused.

CHAPTER TWO

WARNING SIGNS

Whenever Sarah was in a bathroom, she was gripped by a terrifying sense of claustrophobia and anxiety. She began to have trouble closing bathroom doors, even when she needed privacy in public restroom stalls. Sometimes people would walk in on her, but the embarrassment did not prevent her from leaving the door open. When she did force herself to close the stall door, she felt trapped and terribly frightened. She was shocked by her own odd behavior but felt completely out of control.

Sarah was having other problems, too. The anxiety attacks continued to plague her. Without warning, she would be paralyzed by massive anxiety and a sense of impending doom that would last for hours. She had gruesome nightmares, sometimes jumping up and running into the hall in fright while still in the dream state. And depression began to insidiously invade her life, first as a mild, transient state and then as a constant burden of despair and lethargy.

Sarah is a warm, sensitive woman with an open, generous nature. She has an active career as an accountant, a loving marriage, and a much-wanted baby on the way. She was perplexed by the troubling changes in her life. "I know I have some issues to work on in my life, but nothing that seems to account for all these problems. I'm scared. What's happening to me?" Her concerned physician referred her to me for therapy.

Sarah's symptoms indicated the possibility that some unresolved trauma from her past was beginning to surface. The sudden onset of these problems was one clue. She had no previous history of severe depression or anxiety attacks. Her pregnancy could be causing some hormonal problems, but her difficulties began before she was pregnant. She had dealt with family dysfunction and physical abuse by her father in her previous therapy four years ago, but she felt these issues were largely resolved. She also maintained that she had never been happier in her life when these symptoms descended on her, and there was no reason to doubt her perceptions.

The loudest alarm bell that warned of abuse was her odd phobia about closing bathroom stall doors. Such a specific, unusual fear is often linked to a specific, unusual feature of abuse. Bathrooms are used frequently for sexual abuse of children. They provide privacy often lacking in other rooms of the house, and the perpetrator has a ready reason for being undressed if discovered.

Over the course of the next several months, Sarah's symptoms increased. She could no longer stand to have her husband cuddle her spoon-fashion. The feel of his breath on her neck made her want to scream. Her nightmares progressed from generic grisly themes to explicit scenes of child sexual abuse. She also began to cut or nick her hands accidentally whenever she worked with knives in the kitchen. She began to wonder if she was going crazy.

I assured her she was not having any kind of breakdown. Probing her childhood for hidden sources of her current dilemma, however, increased the intensity of her distress, which was an indication that the source of her problems lay buried in the past. As we get closer to what hurts, we hurt more intensely.

POST-TRAUMATIC STRESS: VIETNAM VETS AND SEXUAL ABUSE SURVIVORS

Sarah's troubles suggested a delayed response to childhood abuse called post-traumatic stress disorder, commonly referred to as PTSD. This is a diagnosis used by professionals in the mental health field to describe reactions to severe trauma, including the trauma of sexual abuse. PTSD is not a form of mental illness. It describes a variety of emotional reactions caused by exposure to a terrifying, traumatic event, like war, crime, natural disasters, or child abuse.

PTSD received national attention when returning Vietnam veterans suffered from disturbing reactions to the stress of combat, sometimes beginning long after they had returned from Vietnam. They were tormented by nightmares of their wartime experiences. Flashbacks of terrifying battle scenes were sometimes so real that the ex-soldiers reacted as if these events were happening in the present. Anything that reminded them of battle scenes, like explosive noises, sounds in the darkness, sudden movements, or flashes of lights, could trigger a self-defensive or attack reaction.

The understanding of PTSD gained from Vietnam veterans validated and amplified the work that therapists do with sexual abuse survivors. PTSD offers a nonshaming label for survivors of sexual abuse, one that does not imply that they are crazy or in any way responsible for their abuse. The clear groupings of symptoms verify what therapists are noticing about post-sexual abuse reactions, as well as alerting us to symptoms in survivors that we may otherwise have overlooked.

Education is a vital recovery tool, and understanding the symptoms of PTSD gives many survivors a framework for what they are experiencing. The major symptoms of PTSD are listed in abbreviated form in

Appendix A, with examples related to sexual abuse as needed. To accurately assess whether you have PTSD requires assistance from someone with specialized clinical training, but knowing the symptoms can alert you to seeking that assistance. It can also help you understand what you are going through if you do have PTSD.

Remember that not everyone who has been abused shows PTSD symptoms. Some survivors may never experience symptoms, and others do not notice any symptoms until they are immersed in the process of dealing with their memories. Sometimes the abuse was so prolonged and horrific that the pervasive damage includes far more problems than PTSD reactions.

PTSD AND REPRESSED MEMORIES

PTSD knowledge currently focuses on diagnosing and treating people who remember their abuse. Two characteristics of PTSD are of particular importance for sexual abuse survivors with repressed memories, however. These are the delay in onset of the disorder and amnesia.

Delay in Onset

We know that reactions to sexual abuse can lie quiet for many years. The sexual abuse appears to have left the survivor undamaged until a triggering life event unleashes dormant feelings and memories. Delayed-onset PTSD describes those survivors who suddenly begin to experience PTSD long after the abuse is over.

Triggering events set off delayed-onset PTSD reactions in people who remember their abuse, as well as people who do not remember their abuse. Those who remember their abuse can more easily understand and evaluate the nightmares, images, fears, and other frightening symptoms. The survivors who do not remember often have no idea why they are suddenly having these reactions. They are bewildered at the barrage of their emerging memories.

Delayed-onset PTSD can be triggered by many things. The more common triggering events that survivors experience are listed below. Often a combination of several of these triggering events sets off delayed-onset PTSD.

TRIGGERING EVENTS

1. Unknowingly experiencing a situation that is similar in some way to the original issue. This is the most common trigger, but it is usually not understood until after the abuse memories have been retrieved.
2. Death of a sexually abusive perpetrator or the death of a parent you are unconsciously "protecting" from knowledge of the abuse.
3. Pregnancy or birth of a child or grandchild.
4. A child you identify with reaching the age at which you were abused.
5. Entering a new developmental stage, such as puberty or middle age.
6. Confronting a known sexual abuser. The aftermath of such a confrontation is often the return of memories of abuse by another perpetrator or memories of more severe abuse by the recently confronted perpetrator.
7. Ending an addiction. The addiction to drugs, alcohol, food, gambling, or sex has served to stop the memories from emerging and has medicated the pain caused by the abuse. Without the anesthetizing addiction, memories emerge.

8. Intrusion of the reality of sexual abuse. This can occur through the media, as in a TV special or newspaper story about sexual abuse, or a friend or relative disclosing that they were sexual abused.

9. Feeling safe. You are in a situation where you feel secure enough to finally face the abuse, such as being in therapy with someone capable of addressing the abuse or establishing a supportive primary relationship or friendship.

10. Feeling strong. Personal growth leaves you strong enough to face what could not be faced before. Often this occurs after recovery from dysfunctional family-of-origin issues, like alcoholism or emotional deprivation.

Sarah had three of these triggering events in her life when she began to show PTSD symptoms. She had just married, and she was pregnant with her first child. She also had recently finished therapy to deal with her childhood and family issues, and in her own words, "never felt happier." She was now strong enough to face her repressed memories.

It is possible that Sarah had a fourth triggering event, that of unknowingly being in circumstances that reminded her of the abuse. She experienced her first symptom, an anxiety attack, while walking along with her husband on a bright, sunny day. Memories of abuse might shed light on why the anxiety attack happened at this time.

Amnesia

Including amnesia as a possible response to abuse alerts us to the presence and importance of repressed memories. Nearly all survivors of childhood sexual abuse have some amount of amnesia about their abuse.

They know they were abused, but few, if any, remember each incident in all its detail.

The most disturbing aspects of a sexual assault are the most vulnerable to amnesia. Survivors frequently remember how an incident begins and frequently block out how it ends. The most intrusive sexual acts, the orgasm of the perpetrator, and how the child is treated after the assault are often forgotten. These forgotten segments contain much of the pain of the abuse, and recovery is often incomplete until what is forgotten surfaces and can be confronted.

Nicole believed she remembered more of her sexual abuse. She had been abused as a child, and now was suffering from recurring nightmares about her father molesting her. While awake she sometimes thought she saw him in a crowd, even though he was now dead. She no longer wanted to have sex with her husband, and she felt alienated from everyone around her. She habitually woke up at 3:00 A.M. and had trouble going back to sleep after that. She was often irritable and distracted, especially in the morning.

Nicole had never forgotten that she had been abused by her father. "I can still see him clearly, standing in the darkened doorway of my bedroom, watching me until he thought I was asleep. After a while, I would doze off, and he would come in. I always awoke when he would slowly, carefully pull down the covers, but I pretended to be asleep. Then he would fondle me, squeezing my nipples and rubbing his hand on my genitals."

That was the extent of Nicole's memory of her abuse, but after dealing with her father's molestation, Nicole still showed little improvement. In fact, her PTSD reactions were worsening in intensity. She began having nightmares about being raped, and she frequently thought she saw her father standing in her bedroom door. Intercourse with her husband became an impossibility for her.

In desperation, Nicole decided to try memory recovery work. She began to explore the image of her father standing in her doorway. Slowly and with great sadness, Nicole faced the memory of her father having intercourse with her.

"I hate believing he raped me," she said. "I guess I wanted to hang on to some feeling that he loved me, that he wouldn't do *that* to me. It was so awful to remember how he left me afterward. I was hurting so bad, physically and emotionally, and he treated me like a thing. He wiped me up, never once looking at me, and then walked out of the room. I called to him, and he didn't even hesitate. He just walked out."

As painful as these memories were to confront, Nicole could now finish her grieving. Her symptoms abated, and she experienced a renewed relationship with her husband. What she had forgotten turned out to be just as important as what she remembered.

Highlighting amnesia is essential for survivors like Nicole, who remember that they were sexually abused and need to assess the extent of any amnesia they may have. As it is currently defined, however, PTSD does not adequately describe the effects of memory repression in cases of chronic child abuse. A new category must be developed to describe survivors with repressed memories of abuse.

REPRESSED MEMORY SYNDROME

The repressed memory syndrome was developed to describe those who have no memory of the abuse, as well as those who remember but have a significant amount of amnesia. The syndrome describes symptoms that characterize adults who have repressed memories of abuse, and is more specific to the long-term responses to childhood sexual abuse than PTSD. The repressed memory syndrome consists of four categories: (1) attractions, fears, or avoidances unexplained by known history; (2) indications of emerging memories; (3) evidence of dissociation; (4) time loss or memory blanks.

Please keep in mind that the repressed memory syndrome is only a guide, not an absolute set of criteria. You do not have to have all of the signals, or even one in each of the four areas. Some people will have indicators in all of the areas, while others have a few vague signals in only one area. Some of you have only a feeling that you were abused, but that is enough to begin your journey to find out what happened to you.

Attractions, Fears, or Avoidances Unexplained by Your Known History

Attraction to, avoidance of, or distress around objects or situations unexplained by your known history are warning signs of repressed memories. During sexual abuse, your mind focuses on the events and circumstances surrounding the abuse. You may bury the memory, but you store the reaction to the objects or situations that remind you of the forgotten abuse.

You may want to avoid these reminders, or you may feel some distress around them, like anxiety or nausea. And sometimes there is an odd· attraction or fascination with something that is reminiscent of the abuse, although this certainly does not mean that you liked the abuse. Some of these reactions are noticeable from the time of the abuse to the present, while others start surfacing as a prelude to a memory returning.

Steve believed his mother was sadistic and sexually abusive. One of his first memories to return was of her feeding him in his highchair. "I remember really liking what she was feeding me. I was making pleasure sounds and kicking my feet in anticipation of each bite. Then one bite was suddenly hideous. It was so awful-tasting I started to gag and vomit. Now I think she slipped a spoonful of calf feed into my mouth."

"The strangest thing is," Steve went on, "I've always loved the smell of that calf feed, even though it's the most noxious smell you can imagine." Steve added, "The company that makes it also produces dairy products, and whenever I see that brand in the store I feel a rush of nostalgia. I always buy that brand of butter."

Steve was aptly describing the kind of perverse attraction an abuse survivor can have for something associated with his or her abuse. The association is pleasant not because he liked the abuse but because his pleasurable feelings during the feeding were transferred to the calf supplement. At other times, the association results in a fear or avoidance of the object or event. Unfortunately, the dynamic that causes fear in some cases and attraction in others is unknown.

The fears, attractions, or avoidances are a powerful warning signal if they are about objects or situations that are logically or frequently associated with child sexual abuse. Sex is one such situation, and many survivors have problems with their sex lives as a result of this "reminder factor." Some avoid sex, others become sexually compulsive or overly fascinated with it, and still others feel lots of distress during sex as feelings, flashbacks, or physical reactions intrude on their sexual pleasure.

One survivor, Sheryl, said, "I could never stand to have my husband on top during sex. I always felt horribly crushed, and I had to stifle an urge to scream and rage at him. Now that I have my memories back about my brother laying on me so long after abusing me, I understand why I felt that way."

Although sex is the most obvious reminder, many other objects or situations are also logically or frequently linked with child sexual abuse. Bedrooms, bathrooms, basements, and closets are common places where sexual abuse occurs, so be alert to reactions to those places or to objects in them. Ordinary household items that can be vaginally or anally inserted are often used during abuse, like bottles, sticks, or penis-shaped foods or objects. Extraordinary fear of dental visits is quite often a signal of oral sexual abuse, since it is reminiscent of being forced to open your mouth while something painful is done to it.

It would be impossible to identify all of the things that can remind you of child sexual abuse, so you need to think through any unusual reactions you have. Ask yourself, "Is there anything about this situation or thing I am reacting to that could be associated with sex or sexual abuse?" You may want to also check out what you are reacting to with someone you trust, for denial can make us miss the obvious.

Other things you react to may seem strange to you because they are unique to your abuse and not obviously linked to sex or sexual abuse. Kathy's revulsion toward forks is a good example of this phenomenon. When Kathy retrieved the memory of her aunt putting a fork in her vagina, the origin of her unusual fear was clear.

Marge had an unexplained fondness for an old hairbrush she kept from her childhood. This was unremarkable to her until she remembered her father sexually abusing her with the handle of the brush. Her attachment to this ordinary hairbrush as a "keepsake" was no longer a mystery.

No one knows why survivors of sexual abuse feel an attraction or fascination for something that reminds them of the abuse. Perhaps the positive feelings a survivor is experiencing when the abuse begins shift to some object or aspect of the abuse, rather than evaporating completely. Marge, for example, may have been feeling pleasure in taking her bath and affection for her father when he came in. When he began abusing her, these positive feelings became focused on the bath brush.

Indications of Emerging Memories

Buried memories of abuse intrude into your consciousness through dreams, images, flashbacks, or bodily sensations. They may overwhelm you when you are triggered into remembering abuse, or you may be haunted by the imagery throughout your life. Although you will learn more about retrieving memories using these indicators in later chapters, you need to recognize these warning signals of the existence of repressed memories.

Dreams are often the first sign of emerging memories. Persistent, violent nightmares are a red flag. Also be alert to dreams that involve someone stalking you, chasing you, or trying to murder you, for these are often precursors to emerging repressed memories.

Images, or "blips," are brief flashes of part of a sexual abuse incident that flit through your mind at odd moments. You suddenly get a picture of something unrelated to what you are doing or thinking about, like a flash of a knife or a penis. There is no sense of recall associated with this blip, and it does not seem at all connected to you.

Not all blips are of a violent or abusive nature. Sometimes they are persistent, seemingly innocent images from childhood that are the preserved memory of the beginning or end of an abusive incident. Dave repeatedly said over the course of a year of therapy, "I keep seeing this picture of me as a kid standing on the street corner halfway between my home and the bar my dad owned."

Using hypnosis, he pictured himself walking home, feeling empty and sad, to a bleak scene of his mother drunk and sleeping on the couch. After working with the feelings around this memory, Dave should have been relieved of the persistent image, but it continued to haunt him. Finally, Dave again used hypnosis and retraced his steps back to the bar. He got a clear image of having been sexually abused by one of the bar patrons in the back store room. It was not so much what he was walking home to but what he was walking away from that needed to be faced.

Flashbacks are the sudden reliving of a scene of sexual abuse. In a flashback you actually feel as if the abuse is occurring in the present. Flashbacks are often triggered by graphic descriptions of someone else's abuse, especially if the other person is going through a very emotional retelling of an abusive incident.

Thea was a new member of a therapy group. Another member, Lisa, was describing how her father would make her urinate before sexually abusing her so she would not wet him or the bed during the abuse. Lisa was sobbing as she told in graphic detail how terrified she was of the pain that she knew would follow in her father's ritual of abuse.

Suddenly Thea started shaking and crying out, "No, no! Get away from me! Don't hurt me!" She scrabbled backward and tried to hide behind a chair in the group room. The group calmed her down, reassuring her that she was not being hurt. When she reconnected, she told the group that Lisa's story had triggered a flashback of the elaborate preabuse ritual her father would engage in before raping her.

Bodily feelings of being sexually abused, seeing or hearing abusive scenes, having strong emotional reactions to the topic of sexual abuse, or simply feeling strongly that you were abused are also indicators of repressed memories. Asked if they had ever been sexually abused, clients new to therapy have started crying while saying, "No, why do you ask?" Their emotions are saying something different than their words.

Meg's first indication that she was abused began when hearing a baby crying in a restaurant. Later on the drive home she heard the same thing. She said, "In the restaurant, I thought the crying baby must be out of my sight, but in the car, with the windows rolled up, I knew the crying baby was me."

Evidence of Dissociation

Children dissociate during abuse. After a while, the dissociative state can become a permanent part of their lives, resulting in feelings of unreality, numbness, or estrangement. Even if the memory is lost, the dissociation remains.

Sexual abuse survivors with repressed memories report strong feelings of dissociation. Karen described her sense of dissociation as the feeling that "everyone but me is real." Shelley said, "Anything is better than this numbness. When I cut my arms, at least I feel something." Ken felt totally unconnected to anyone. "My isolation is my prison and my refuge," he said. "I trade my safety for my loneliness."

Sometimes the dissociation is not a general state of being but a reaction to anything that is reminiscent of the forgotten abuse. Again, sexual relationships are especially vulnerable to dissociation because sex is a reminder of sexual abuse. Going through a sexual encounter as if you are "not there" is common for survivors with repressed memories.

Time Loss or Memory Blanks

Sometimes there are clear time losses or memory blanks that indicate the possibility of sexual abuse. If you remember almost nothing or very little of your childhood, or if you cannot remember a period of time, such as between the ages of ten and fourteen, you have repressed memories. People do not block out years of their lives for some small trauma, or because of a sense of general unhappiness. Time is lost only for very painful reasons.

· Another form of memory loss is blocking a significant person out of your life. Molly, for example, has no memories of her grandfather, who lived next door to her family until his death when she was five. She does remember her grandmother, though, as well as many significant and insignificant incidents from her preschool years. This information indicates the need to explore the role her grandfather played in her life.

EMPOWERING YOURSELF

The following is a checklist of symptoms that many survivors with buried memories have experienced. It is not a complete list of reactions, by any means, for each person's abuse and the things they react to are so unique. The list does highlight common warning signals of repressed memories. It may also prompt you to notice unusual reactions in areas you had not thought of before.

Check each item that applies to you, even if in a different way than the question indicates. There is no specific number of checkmarks needed to "prove" you have repressed memories. This list is only to help you start thinking about warning signals you may have missed or to validate signals that you feel might be clues to your abuse.

No single item is a certain indicator of repressed memories. People who have not been sexually abused have nightmares, overeat, and sometimes hate their bodies, but if you check several times in each category, or nearly all the items in a single category, you will want to consider the possibility that you have repressed memories. Talk over your responses with a therapist if you feel concerned about the number of items you have checked, or any checked item that particularly bothers you.

SYMPTOM CHECKLIST

Sexuality
1. I began masturbating at a very early age.
2. As a child, I used to insert objects into my bottom, and I do not know where I learned to do this.
3. I seemed to know some things about sex even before they were explained to me.
4. I showed no interest in sex until I was in my twenties.
5. I can't stand to be touched in certain sexual ways or on areas of my body.
6. My experiences with sex are degrading or short-lived.
7. I freeze up or can't say no when someone wants to be sexual with me.
8. I have a sexual dysfunction, such as premature ejaculation, inability to have an orgasm, or pain during intercourse.
9. I am preoccupied with thoughts about sex.
10. I feel as if there is something wrong or bad about my sexuality.
11. There is only one way I can have an orgasm or one position that turns me on.
12. I have fantasies of sexual abuse during sex.
13. I have had a period of sexual promiscuity in my life.

Sleep
1. I often have nightmares.
2. I have difficulty falling or staying asleep.

3. I sometimes wake up feeling as if I am choking, gagging, or being suffocated.
4. Sometimes I fear or sense that someone is in my bedroom.
5. I had or have recurring dreams.
6. I remember vividly one or more nightmares from my childhood.
7. I have awakened from sleep trying to attack my partner.
8. I often wake up frightened at the same time every night.

Fears and Attractions
1. I am frightened of one or more common household objects.
2. I would never go into a closet or any dark, confined space.
3. Basements terrify me.
4. There are certain things I seem to have a strange affection or attraction for.
5. I am scared to be alone or to leave my house.
6. I hate going to the dentist more than most people.
7. I neglect my teeth.
8. My mouth seems repulsive to me.
9. I hate to have someone touch my hair.
10. I am always alert to the possibility of sexual assault.
11. I have often taken foolish risks with my safety.

Eating Disturbances
1. I have had periods in my life when I couldn't eat, or I had to force myself to eat.
2. Sometimes I binge on huge amounts of food.
3. Certain foods or tastes frighten me or nauseate me.
4. I am seriously underweight or overweight.

5. I gag or choke easily.
6. I make myself throw up, take laxatives, or exercise exhaustively to control my weight.

Body Problems
1. I do not take good care of my body.
2. I hate my body.
3. I have odd sensations in my genitals or rectum.
4. I avoid going to a gynecologist, or I dread it terribly.
5. Whenever I think of a certain person from my childhood, I get a sensation in my genitals.

Compulsive Behaviors
1. I sometimes hurt myself in a way that marks or scars my body.
2. I have an addiction to drugs or alcohol.
3. My drug or alcohol use started before I was thirteen.
4. I do some things to excess and I just don't know when to quit.
5. I pick at my body too much.
6. I can't seem to control myself when it comes to spending money or gambling.

Emotional Signals
1. There have been times when I was very suicidal.
2. I feel a sense of doom, as though my life will end in tragedy or disaster.
3. I have unexplained bouts of depression.
4. I have a strong sense that something terrible has happened to me.
5. I identify with abuse victims in the media, and often stories of abuse make me want to cry.
6. The pain in my life seems too big compared to what I know has happened to me.

7. Nothing seems very real sometimes.
8. I am not in touch with my feelings; I am usually numb.
9. Sometimes really violent or strange pictures flash through my mind.
10. I startle easily.
11. I can't remember much of my childhood.
12. There is a blank period in my childhood when I can remember nothing.
13. Other people seem to have childhood memories at an earlier age than I do.
14. I space out or daydream.

CHAPTER THREE

HOW COULD I FORGET?

*Sarah was shocked and disbelieving when I suggested that
her symptoms were perhaps related to unremembered sexual abuse. "I have an excellent memory," she asserted.
"I remember more of my childhood than most of my
friends. Small things that happened to me as a little girl
stand out so clearly that they seem etched in my memory.
How could I remember these in so much detail and forget
something as momentous as abuse?*

*"I know I was physically abused by my father, and I
recall that abuse clearly. If I were abused in other ways,
I'm certain I would remember that, too. At least there
would be some feeling inside me that this was real, some
sense that someone had hurt me badly. It just can't be
true."*

Sarah's reliance on her excellent memory led her to
harbor the belief that she could not possibly block out a
major trauma. She remembers other painful experiences
with startling clarity, so it seemed as if abuse is the last
thing she would forget. The only forgetting she feels
familiar with is the repression of trivial, mundane information that is irritating to be unable to recall. She mistakenly believed that her reliable memory makes her
immune to repression.

The accuracy of her memory is unrelated to whether
or not she has repressed memories. Repression is a survival technique associated with abuse, and it is not
linked to the capacity for accurate recall. People with

repressed memories run the gamut from those with for-
getful, patchy memories to those, like Sarah, who have
preserved much of their past and nearly all of their present in their conscious minds.

Sarah also had no sense of missing pieces in the
puzzle of her life. She believed that anything as earth-
shaking as child abuse would leave some sort of
memory trace, some accessible, lasting impression.
This kind of blind spot is not uncommon. While some
victims of abuse feel throughout their lives that something is very wrong, others have no awareness of repressing a traumatic childhood memory. For them,
the abuse memory emerges as an entirely new, shocking reality.

Sarah is facing something that is both frightening
and foreign to her. At first glance, memory repression
seems to be a bizarre, obscure occurrence. In reality, it
is an expedient, rational defense against a memory that
would dramatically diminish a child's capacity to survive and flourish.

UNDERSTANDING
MEMORY REPRESSION

Memory repression may seem a bit farfetched at first
glance. You may view it as something that only happens to strange, disturbed people from families on the
lunatic fringe. You may think that nothing so extraordinary could be a part of your past.

Most people who have repressed memories are not
odd or weird. As a matter of fact, most are models of
normalcy. This form of amnesia lurks in the background of millions of ordinary, high-functioning
Americans. If you already know you have been abused
or if you have some of the warning signals given in
Chapter Two, you probably do have repressed memo-

ries. You are unlikely to be the exception to the rule, no matter what your denial is telling you.

Knowing the basic elements of how memories are repressed will provide you with an outline to follow in reclaiming your memories. Once you know how memory repression works, you will be better able to piece your reactions and symptoms into a meaningful picture that shows what happened to you. Confusing clues about your abuse will fall into place much more easily.

Memory repression is the creative product of a convergence of factors. It is not a single moment of memory slippage. It is multifaceted, set in motion before the abuse happens, shaped profoundly during the abuse, and reinforced by the perpetrator and family afterward.

SETTING THE STAGE: BEFORE THE ABUSE

The seeds of memory repression are sown long before abuse happens. Predisposing factors set up a child to develop amnesia and influence the degree of amnesia present. Age of the child, hypnotizability, and a family history of memory repression make a child vulnerable to memory repression.

Age of the Child

Think back over your childhood. Notice that you can remember so much more of your high school years than you can of your elementary school years. Your toddler and preschool memories are probably very sparse, and your infancy memories are nonexistent. Your ability to retain and recall events is something that developed over the course of your childhood.

The younger the child, the more vulnerable he or she is to memory repression. This is not to say that abuse amnesia cannot happen to older children or even adults. It can and it does. Younger children, however, lack recall ability, verbal skills, and sophisticated thought processes to order their reality. Forgetting is sometimes the only defense available against abuse for the very young.

Helen had repressed memories from her infancy and early childhood. In working to recover a memory of sexual abuse when she was two, she had a brief flash of someone putting a pencil in her bottom. Suddenly she burst into tears and said, "Why does he want to touch my potty parts? He hurted me." When Helen let herself speak as a little child, she poignantly revealed the difficulty a two-year-old mind has in grasping and communicating the horrifying reality of sexual abuse.

You probably have doubts about the ability of infants and toddlers being able to remember their abuse. As difficult as it is to believe, abuse memories from early infancy have often been corroborated by other family members, witnesses, or medical evidence. Therapists with extensive experience in repressed memories have many cases in which the infant abuse memories are confirmed by other data.

Beth, for example, had persistent images of a three-month-old being placed on a table, her diaper taken off, and an old man pounding his hands on the table on either side of her head as he ejaculated on her. Her grandfather had been sexually abusive to her mother, and her mother had worked with her own repressed memories in therapy. Beth asked her mother to come in for a session to tell her about the imagery.

Before describing the image, Beth asked her mother if her grandfather had ever had access to her. Beth's mother answered, "I left her with my dad once, when she was three months old, to visit my mom in the hospital. I remember because I had changed her, fed her, and put her down for a nap, and, when I came home, my dad had changed her diaper. I had only been gone

for forty-five minutes. The used diaper was laying on
the kitchen table, and it didn't even look wet. I've never
forgotten that incident, even after twenty years."

A baby does have ways of remembering abusive incidents, and the adult can access those memories. A
colleague, Cheryl Beardslee, coined the phrase "infant
trauma memory" to account for the sexually abused
children who were able to relate details about abuse in
their infancy. Many times their shocked parents confirmed the accuracy of the children's details, saying
things like, "I have no idea how she knew that!"

Hypnotizability

Repression of memories usually involves some elements of hypnosis. During abuse, children react to the
shock by going into a trance state that distances them
from reality. They will often use self-hypnotic suggestions to further separate themselves from the abuse.
How easily you can be hypnotized is an important predisposing factor in memory repression.

Some adults make excellent hypnotic subjects, while
others cannot be hypnotized at all. This great variance
in hypnotizability led Sigmund Freud to abandon it as
his primary method of psychotherapy and to develop
free association as "the talking cure"instead. Differences
in hypnotizability account for its limited usefulness in
such areas as pain control, stopping smoking, or weight
control.

Children vary as much as adults in their individual
hypnotizability. In order to successfully use the defense
of memory repression, a child must have some ability
to enter a trance state. The more a child is able to dissociate and enter a trance-like state, the more likely he
or she is to use memory repression as a way to deal with
the cruel reality of the abuse.

Of course, if you were a small child when the abuse
happened, or if the abuse was painful enough, you bur-

ied at least some of your memories of it, no matter how poor a hypnotic subject you are. Also, many survivors are extremely poor hypnotic subjects now because they fear reexperiencing a state that is associated with the pain and distress of their abuse.

A Family History of Memory Repression

Bill remembered his grandfather as a constant and expert whittler. He even had a toy gun his grandpa whittled for him. When Bill recovered memories of his grandfather assaulting him and using the whittling knife to threaten him, he decided to tell his father.

"I was pretty sure he would want to know that his dad had done this horrible thing to me. When I told him, he believed me and was pretty supportive. But when I told him about Grandpa using his whittling knife to silence me, my dad told me he had no memory of Grandpa ever whittling! If I didn't still have that beautifully crafted wooden gun, I would think I was crazy. Obviously, my dad has repressed memories too."

Like so many family issues, the repression of memories runs in families. If you have repressed memories of abuse, it is very likely that one or both of your parents do too. Heredity, learning, and family system rules all combine to pass on memory repression of abuse as an odd "family tradition."

DURING THE ABUSE

Powerful forces coalesce during the abuse to pressure children to forget. Even if they remember some of what happens, they will certainly forget other parts of the experience. Survival mechanisms kick in to protect them as their senses are bombarded with pain, shock, and sexual stimuli they are unprepared to experience.

Painful or Bizarre Abuse

Abuse that is either too painful or too bizarre for the child to cope with necessitates the protection of amnesia. The physical pain may be intense, and far too much for a child's mind or body to bear. The abuse may be extremely discrepant with the world the child normally lives in, or a normally sane, trusted person may act in a way that is freakish and completely unfamiliar.

Colleen was only three when her grandmother began to fondle her genitals whenever she slept overnight with her. Sometimes she put things like pencils and bobby pins in Colleen's bottom and hurt her. In the middle of the night, Colleen's nice, comfy grandma changed into a heavy-breathing, mean, sweaty person, and then changed back again in the morning. How easy it was for Colleen to resolve the problem by believing only in her "good grandma" and forgetting her "bad grandma" ever existed.

Do not be fooled by those who cannot look at the suffering of children honestly and who claim that abuse does not damage. Abuse always involves pain. If the abuse is physical, there is pain and the betrayal of safety and nurturance. If the abuse is sexual, there is pain, betrayal, and the shameful, bewildering manipulation of a child's body. Most sexual abuse is physically painful for children in some manner, but even if there is no physical pain, a child will be badly damaged by the sheer horror of what is happening.

Some people find direct comfort in believing that if sexual assault is not physically painful, or if the child is too young to understand what happened, there is no trauma for the child. This is not true. Too many babies under two years of age react with heartbreaking distress to anything that reminds them of their sexual abuse, even when they have not been physically hurt during the assault.

A psychology experiment with rats can help you understand this phenomenon. In the study, university students were given rats to feed, care for, and run in automatically timed mazes. One group of students was told that their rats were maze bright, bred specifically to figure out mazes quickly, while another group was told their rats were maze dull, bred to run mazes slowly.

In fact, the rats used in the study were neither maze bright nor maze dull. They were bred from an average strain of laboratory rats, and they should have run the mazes in nearly identical times. But the rats the students thought were maze bright actually ran the mazes significantly faster than the rats the students thought were maze dull.

If rats can pick up expectations about running mazes, how much more sensitive are children, however young, to the sickness of an act of child sexual abuse? During sexual abuse, children feel and incorporate the rage, pain, shame, and sense of perversion that the perpetrator is projecting. They take these feelings into the very core of themselves, and they are badly traumatized by the emotions surrounding the assault, as well as by the assault itself.

Dissociation

Dissociation gets you through a brutal experience, letting your basic survival skills operate unimpeded. For a brief time you are protected from full comprehension of the danger you are in. Your ability to survive is enhanced as the ability to feel is diminished. You can do what you otherwise could not do under even optimal conditions.

Dissociation always occurs during abuse, because abuse is always traumatic. The abusive act is too painful or too frightening for you to experience. All feelings are blocked; you "go away." You are disconnected from the act, the perpetrator, and yourself.

"I get this picture of a girl lying in a bed and a man lying next to her, touching her," Kathy explained. "I see it from above, like I'm on the ceiling looking down at the scene. The picture comes into my head at the oddest times. I can't say I feel bad about it. I don't have any feelings about it at all. It just bothers me because it's so strange."

Kathy is describing a classic example of a dissociated image of sexual abuse. Her numbness about a horrifying, intrusive mental picture is a sure indicator that she is in a dissociative state. She is disconnected from her feelings, her body, and even her perceptions of the assault. Viewing the scene from up above, or some other out-of-body perspective, is common among sexual abuse survivors.

Dissociation, a form of hypnotic trance, helps children survive abuse, and it is key to memory repression. The abuse takes on a dream-like, surreal quality, and deadened feelings and altered perceptions add to the strangeness. The whole scene does not fit into the "real world." It is simple to forget, easy to believe nothing happened.

Abusers are usually dissociated during the abuse, too. They are aware of what they are doing and are caught up in some sort of feeling state, like rage or sexual arousal, but they are disconnected from their relationship with the child and their sense of self. For example, Colleen's "bad grandma" was so dissociated from anything except her sexual arousal that she seemed like a different person to Colleen than her "good grandma." Her grandmother's dissociation lent an even greater unreality to the bizarre scene, pushing Colleen further toward memory repression.

Dissociation offers sorely needed protection to a child at a perpetrator's mercy, but it can become a permanent state. The abuse can occur so often that one episode of dissociation blends into another. The child begins to exist in a numb emotional state. Kindergarten, sunshine, playtime, friendships, everything becomes suffused with a feeling of unreality. If they repress all memory of abuse, they grow up knowing only inexplicable pain and a sense of detachment from the essence of life.

Refocusing

While in the trance-like state that is dissociation, children also focus on some surrounding detail to distract themselves from the appalling situation they are in. Focusing on some object, thought, or sensory experience as a distractor in an autohypnotic technique. It is commonly suggested to women in labor as a method of pain control. For abused children, focusing on something, like the wallpaper, the sound of the wind, or the fantasy of mother coming to the rescue, heightens the dissociative state. The pain of the abuse is numbed and overshadowed by whatever is focused on.

Al remembers only fragments of his abuse. When his oldest brother would corner him in the basement, Al would panic, running desperately in circles while his brother laughed at him. "Bob would close in, and I would start to smell his breath. It always smelled like rotten meat. I would hate and hate and *hate* his breath all the time he was touching me. It was all I could think about. I know it sounds crazy, but I hated his bad breath more than I hated whatever he was doing to me."

Al's refocusing on his brother's bad breath helped him block the shame and pain of being molested and anally abused. When he does memory work, he only can surface brief flashes of the sexual abuse before he begins to focus on the smell. Al is also obsessed with the fear that he has bad breath, sometimes using so much mouthwash that the inside of his mouth breaks out in sores.

Hypnotic Suggestion

Children being abused often engage in a form of self-hypnosis during the abuse. They repeat over and over to themselves sentences like, "I made it up, I made it up" or "This isn't happening, this isn't happening." The repetition of sentences like these is a hypnotic suggestion to the child, like the parlor hypnotist repeating, "You are getting sleepy," to induce a trance. These repetitions are powerful commands to distrust reality and to forget what happened.

Marilyn has recovered most of her memories. She even remembers the self-hypnosis she used to bury her memories. "After every assault, I would tell myself over and over that I was dreaming. It made the pain and the fear go away. After a while, I got better and better at saying it and making the whole thing fade really quickly. Pretty soon I believed I just had these terrible, awful nightmares. I couldn't even remember for sure what they were about."

The abuser sometimes adds to the hypnotic suggestions by telling children they made it up or are dreaming. A compelling message from someone who has you completely in his power is a potent influence. Marilyn's father would silence her when she would start to protest by stroking her hair and saying softly, "Hush, now, you're just having a bad dream. Sleep. Sleep."

Sedation with Drugs and Alcohol

Abusers sometimes give children drugs or alcohol to quiet them during the abuse or in the hopes that the children will not remember what happened. It is a surprisingly common factor in memory repression. Unless enough is given to completely anesthetize them, however, the children often retain a hazy memory of the abuse.

Tammy was a four-year-old victim of a sex ring.

Her natural father was fighting to protect his daughter from sexual abuse by her mother and her friends, who were heavy drug users. After weekends at home with her mother, Tammy would describe odd scenes of cameras, lights, and penises all jumbled together. Whenever she would talk about this, she would change from being alert to being very drowsy, with her eyes drooping and her speech mumbly and slow. Afterward, she would act normally again.

The mystery was solved, sadly enough, when Tammy's father picked her up from a visit with her mother and saw that Tammy was in this drowsy state. He took her immediately to a hospital, where she tested positive for a mild sedative. He was able to protect her from being used in further films or photos. She is only one example of the harsh reality of drugging children for sexual purposes.

Most adults who were drugged as children were not survivors of sex rings. More often a single perpetrator "spikes" the child's food, drink, or baby bottle with alcohol or available prescription drugs. Many of the survivors reexperience the drugged lethargy when they get in touch with their memories, just as Tammy did.

When Jerry first recovered his memories, he would complain of feeling very sleepy afterward, which he thought was just an emotional reaction to the stress of remembering. He also recalled many mornings as a child when he would wake up so lethargic he could barely dress himself. He wrote this off as being "shell-shocked" from the sexual abuse of the night before. When he recovered a memory of his father holding his head and forcing him to drink something before he went to sleep, the pieces fell into place. He knew he was drugged by his father during nocturnal sexual assaults.

AFTER THE ABUSE

Rescue is always abused children's first choice for protection from further abuse. After the abusive incident is over, they may try to preserve the memory to tell to someone, anyone, in the hope that they will be protected. But the family and the perpetrator let them know in the aftermath of abuse that there is no one to tell, no one to help. The need to forget is powerfully reinforced. If rescue is not possible, the children want nothing more than to forget.

Normalization

The reaction of the family gives survivors a strong push in the direction of memory repression. After the abuse the perpetrator and the family behave normally, as if nothing happened. No one notices the distress of the child or any telltale signs. The hushed silence or excited chatter that is the aftermath of a major crisis is completely absent.

Nadine is a victim of sixteen years of sexual abuse by her father. She described normalization clearly: "It was so awful to get up the next morning, stunned and hurting from all the things my dad had done to me in the night, and see him flipping pancakes, humming and smiling. And my mom would act like a TV mom, urging us kids to eat a good breakfast. We would sit around the breakfast table like the Waltons, everyone but me laughing and chattering. No wonder it was so easy to forget it ever happened."

Denial

Denial is acting as if what you know is not true, and it is a potent force in the repression of memories. Denial confuses people about what is real and what is not real. When the family denies what the abused child says or does to let them know he or she was abused, the child's fragile sense of reality is even further undermined.

Sometimes the denial involves not noticing and is part of the normalization process. Nadine's family never noticed her subdued demeanor at the breakfast table, and no one ever mentioned the semen stains on her pajamas or bedsheets. Denial added to the unreality of Nadine's abuse, as she began to trust the family pretense instead of her own reality.

Sometimes denial is more direct. Stan remembers the time he told his mother about the baby-sitter abusing him. "I told her Sandy was touching my privates and I didn't like it. I was scared, but I was sure she would help me. Instead she got mad and told me I shouldn't ever make things up like that. She stayed mad at me all afternoon. The whole thing already seemed so strange and unreal to me that I just buried it away and tried never to think about it. That worked for sixteen years. Now I think about it all the time."

No matter what the parent actually says, there is always a covert message that comes through loud and clear. When a child tells and is ignored or contradicted, the underlying message is: "Just forget it ever happened." No one listens to the child, but the child listens to the covert message and obeys it.

Repetition of Suggestions to Forget

You've probably seen comedy shows where a person is hypnotized to act like a chicken whenever a bell rings. Hilarity ensues when the hypnotized person clucks and struts whenever a bell rings in the most inappropriate situations. He is responding to a post-hypnotic suggestion.

A not-so-funny version of post-hypnotic suggestion happens to abused children. Thoughts, feelings, or pictures of the abuse flash into their minds long after the abuse is over. Whenever these flashes return, the children feel anxious and push them away by repeating whatever self-hypnotic suggestions they used during the abuse, like "You're making it up." The repetitions serve as post-hypnotic suggestions, hammering home the message to forget.

EMPOWERING YOURSELF

In applying this information to your own life, you may want to ask yourself the questions listed below. Record the answers in your journal or simply tune into your reactions to increase your awareness of your inner reality. Not all of the questions will apply to you, but as they say in Twelve-Step groups, "Take what you like and leave the rest."

Age of the child. How old do you think you were when you were first abused? Write down the very first number that pops into your head, no matter how improbable it seems to you, even if it is very different than the age you previously believed or suspected. Does it seem too young to be true? I assure you it is not.

Hypnotizability. Do you think you would be a good hypnotic subject? Do you or others in your life consider you suggestible? Do you "space out" often? Or do you have a strong fear of being hypnotized? Does the thought of being under another person's control or power seem particularly noxious to you?

Family history of memory repression. Do you sense or believe that your parents were abused, even though they deny any abuse in their past? Do your parents show any signs of sexual abuse? Do you have any data that might suggest your parents have repressed memories?

Painful or bizarre abuse. Have you experienced bizarre or painful sexual abuse that you know of? Do you think you have all your abuse memories back yet? Do you show some of the warning signs in Chapter Two?

Dissociation. Do you often experience feelings of un-reality? Do you have flashes or imagery of abuse but lack much feeling about these flashes? Do you live your life alternately feeling empty and in unexplained pain, with most other feelings blocked?

Sedation. Do you feel sleepy or lethargic when you have a memory or image of abuse? Do some of the scenes of abuse you remember seem jumbled or confusing? Do you have a hatred that you do not understand for the smell of alcohol or the idea of taking pills?

Hypnotic suggestion, during and after. Is there a sentence you routinely say to yourself when you have an abuse-related flash, imagery, or dream? If not, does one come to mind now? What is it?

Normalization. Do you sometimes doubt your memories or suspicions because your family or perpetrator was too "normal" for sexual abuse? Does your family respond to crises with a "business-as-usual" attitude?

Denial. Did your parents usually notice when you were distressed or upset and inquire about it? Is there a history of denial in your family about other problems, like chemical abuse, depression, or feelings in general?

CHAPTER FOUR

THE FAMILY SYSTEM: UNTOLD LIES

Sarah knew her uncle had sexually abused his younger sister. Now she began to suspect her grandfather, the father of this uncle and aunt, of abusing her brutally from infancy until his death when she was four. Her suspicion alternated with her doubts.

"I don't remember my grandfather, but my family talks about him as being the farthest thing from a sadist. He was always described as so meek and mild. They say he was a soft-spoken dreamer whose plans never quite got off the ground. My dad says he was one of the nicest guys he ever met.

"My family doesn't seem to have the depth of pain and destruction you would expect to find with the severity of abuse I am picturing. I must be making it up. My relatives are all stable, law-abiding citizens. Oh, sure, there are a few alcoholics and some depressed people, but most of them are high-achieving professionals and caring family types.

"The sexual abuse by my uncle doesn't fit either. My aunt told me it involved exploratory fondling when my uncle was a teenager and she was a little girl. It wasn't at all brutal or violent. The whole thing just doesn't add up."

The more Sarah revealed about her family, the more confusing her imagery and symptoms seemed. The family certainly sounded dysfunctional, but the level of dysfunction did not match the level of abuse she was remembering. Only my experience with the power of a family to keep sickness a secret helped me remain open to the possibility that her images were real.

Then Sarah had a dream in which she encountered a disreputable, multigenerational incest family in a fast food restaurant. She inadvertently discovered that the entire family was colluding in the grandfather's sexual torture of the youngest child. Sarah's dream-self intervened to save the toddler, and the incest family had her arrested on undefined but ominous charges. She was terrified during the Kafka-like trial, especially as the family members began lying about her conduct and manipulating the judges for sympathy.

The dream seemed to be representative of Sarah's struggle to rescue herself from a denying, guilting family system, but the end of the dream pointed toward a deeper level of meaning. Sarah said, "The judges started talking, and it was crystal clear that each one of them perceived the family as it really was—abusive, conniving, and dishonest. I suddenly felt so safe and so validated."

The dream indicated that Sarah was now ready to see her family system in a new light. I asked her to list her maternal aunts and uncles and to describe anything aberrant about them. The information she gave jolted both of us.

Her mother, the oldest, was prone to dark depressions. The second oldest, who had abused his younger sister, was a young man who apparently died of alcohol poisoning when he was twenty and was rumored to have been sniffing or drinking gasoline on the day he died. The next sister was impoverished and married to an alcoholic who made his living selling drugs to his children and their friends in a small town.

The most "normal" uncle lived an upwardly mobile lifestyle, but both he and his wife were extremely emotionally and verbally abusive, at least to Sarah. Another uncle was abnormally protective of his oldest daughter during her teenage years, never allowing her to leave the house except for school, and one of his sons sexually abused the younger sisters.

The youngest daughter, the one who had been sexually abused by her brother, lived in an appallingly filthy house and was married to a man who demanded sex at least once a day. The youngest son died in his early thirties from unknown causes. Sarah was told by her aunt that he tried to torture and mutilate animals.

None of this information had been forgotten or recently acquired. Sarah simply had a filter for her family that permitted a view from only one perspective. She saw a hardworking, family-oriented group of people that she grew up admiring, loving, and laughing with. The kaleidoscope shifted, and she suddenly saw an incest family, complete with abusers, alcoholics, and emotionally damaged people.

THE ABUSIVE FAMILY SYSTEM

Most of you come into therapy with a view of your family that is rosy. Like Sarah, you view your family as being too healthy to account for how bad you are feeling or for the horrifying memories that are emerging. When the family myth is questioned, no matter how gently, the family image is defended vociferously.

In reality, the health of a family system bears absolutely no relationship to either its public image or the sincerity of your beliefs about its normalcy. A facade of normalcy can convincingly cover anything from mild dysfunction to the most horrendous child abuse imaginable. The abusive family system is a family in camouflage.

The conspicuously abusive family, where the parents are rageful and cruel and the children are dirty, bruised, and frightened, represents only one percent of all abusive families. The rest of abusive families look like all the other typical American families. The parents hold down decent jobs, dress and speak appropriately, and the family fits in well in the community. The children do well in school, have friends, and go about the normal activities of growing up in America. Even if a family is not highly regarded, it blends into the background along with millions of other families, invisible to anyone scrutinizing for abuse.

The abuse is not only hidden from public view but from the view of the family members themselves. The family members believe the facade of normalcy because it is what they have grown up with. Anything that does not fit is buried or rationalized away. Anyone who tells the secrets or points out the sickness is punished or even exiled. The facade is maintained at the expense of individual family members.

The facade may or may not be true, but it functions to keep you from looking at the abuse in your family to retrieve memories. To explore the truth of your past, you need to suspend belief in the family myth of normalcy. You need to look below the surface to the underlying family structure.

THE OVERT AND COVERT SYSTEMS IN FAMILIES

Abusive families have two systems: the overt system and the covert system. The two systems operate simul-

taneously but independently from one another. Anyone
who has worked in a company with lots of "office pol-
itics" has firsthand experience with overt and covert
systems. When you first start the job, you are only
aware of the overt system. The staff appears friendly,
competent, productive, and progressive. Underneath,
destructive mind-games, vicious power plays, and ex-
clusionary alliances are in operation.

The Overt System

In families, everyday activities, like play, meals, TV
watching, household chores, bedtime rituals, and family celebrations, make up the overt system. The family
members are immersed in the overt level on a daily
basis, and they bond to each other at this level. They
feel love, affection, and loyalty not only for each other
but also for the image of the family as caring, strong,
and devoted.

Belief in the overt system is so strong that it is difficult to believe repressed abuse memories when they
emerge. The family at first appears so accomplished, so
stodgy, or so wholesome that it seems impossible for
anything perverse to ever have occurred. The family
myth of normalcy is extremely powerful.

The Covert System and Sexual Abuse

Sooner or later, the covert system is exposed in the
recovery process. It contains the secrets, the shame,
the weaknesses, the hidden hopes and dreams, and the
deepest emotional forces that sweep through the family.
It is the level of family life that no one talks about but
everyone senses.

Sexual abuse always occurs at this covert level of
family functioning. It is a secret, having tremendous
impact on the family but hidden from the outside
world. Family members may or may not be consciously
aware of the abuse, but even if they do know about it,

they do not speak it. Everyone knows when to disappear, what not to question, and when to look away. All are aware, at some level, of the pain and the no-talk rule about the abuse.

Linda described the overt and covert systems in her family with deep bitterness. "We were the all-American family. We were supposed to be so close and loving. We had family meetings once a week where we talked about family decisions and conflicts. But when my dad wanted to rape me, everyone fled. I don't know how they knew or where they went, but everyone would just somehow leave the house. He would chase me, rip my clothes off, and in all those years, all that abuse, never once did anyone walk in on him accidently."

Later Linda found out that her father had also been raping her sister. Just like the rest of her family, Linda knew the covert system well enough to disappear and not to intrude during her father's sexual assaults on her sister. Never once were she or her sister able to signal each other about their shared experience.

The Covert System and Repressed Memories

Even the most apparently healthy family can have depths of sickness that astound outsiders. The resulting confusion from these conflicting realities encourages memory repression. The greater the discrepancy between the overt system and the covert system, the greater the likelihood of memory repression.

Remember Colleen's "good grandma" who was kind to her during the day but would turn into the "bad grandma" at night during the sexual abuse? The easiest way for Colleen to deal with two such different grandmothers is to forget the "bad grandma." The pressure to forget is even greater, however, if her "good grandma" is a sweet, compassionate woman who is active in her church, known for helping neighbors in trouble, and married to the kindly town doctor.

Ned sought therapy because he suffered from powerful homicidal urges, severe depression, and persistent anxiety attacks. He also reported seeing images that portrayed his mother and father together masturbating on him and with him when he was an infant. To Ned, the images were so bizarre they were preposterous.

His family was socially prominent and considered above reproach. He brought pictures of his family to therapy, and they appeared to be an exceptionally attractive, lighthearted clan. "Look," he said, gesturing to the photos. "How could anyone believe these children were raised by sexual freaks?"

Ned's description of his father added to the implausibility of his memories. "My father is one of the most successful trial lawyers this city has ever seen. He is not just respected, he is esteemed by the legal profession here. These images must be symbolic of the emotional deprivation I experienced as a youngster. They couldn't be real."

When Ned's older brother was hospitalized after a suicide attempt, Ned visited him. His brother confided that he had been troubled by memories of their father and mother sexually abusing him. The two brothers shared their stories and found them remarkably similar. Their father was living a double life, impervious to public scrutiny. "He almost fooled us," Ned said, tearfully. "We both could have lived our lives feeling crazy, never knowing the truth."

When the overt and covert systems are extremely discrepant, it is not only more likely that memory repression will occur but it is also more difficult to believe the memories once they are retrieved. The emerging repressed memories seem bizarre in comparison to the overt system. Survivors must then struggle against their own crippling disbelief and overwhelming family censure.

Sherry's father is an English professor at a prestigious New England college. He is an articulate teacher, well-loved by the students. "Over and over again he is selected for the teacher-of-the-year award," she told me. "Everyone loves him, including my family. Including me! I find it so hard to believe that he could sexually abuse me. My sisters tell me I'm insane to even think such thoughts, and most of the time I think they're right."

Sherry's father has the charisma and charm often found in sexual perpetrators. Only over the course of several years of painfully slow therapy was Sherry able to penetrate his facade. Evidence that he was at times cruel and sexually compulsive emerged first from Sherry's memories. His pornography "stash," his sexually demeaning tirades against women, and his verbal abuse of her mother finally convinced Sherry that he was not straight out of *Father Knows Best.*

Sherry decided to believe her memories without constantly questioning herself. She wanted to find out how she would feel if she trusted herself at every level. She was overjoyed to find that after only a few months she had more confidence than she had ever had before. "It's like someone turned on a light," she said. "Now I find it hard to believe I ever trusted him and distrusted myself."

Sherry's journey to her own reality was long and arduous, but her story also illustrates the importance of exposing and believing what is happening in the covert system. The greater the discrepancy between the overt and covert systems, the greater the relief and recovery when abuse is uncovered. Survivors like Sherry and Ned find the struggle well worth the effort.

FAMILY ROLES

The covert system in sexually abusive families has certain commonalities that are recognizable to any survivor. Each family member is in one of three roles: offender, denier, or victim. All three of these roles are a learned response to living in a sexually abusive family system.

Roles in families are comparable to jobs in a work situation. In a restaurant, for example, the available work roles are boss, cook, waiter, and cleanup person. These work roles are filled by people of various personalities with the necessary abilities to do the job. A need exists and people perform the necessary function. For a family to be sexually abusive, people must fulfill the roles of victim, denier, and offender.

The *term* victim generally means that someone has been victimized. The *role* of victim, however, means not only that a person has been victimized but that he or she performs the role of victim in his family as well. In sexually abusive families, people in the victim role have all been sexually abused. Their response to the sexual abuse over time is the learned powerlessness of the victim role.

The roles of denier and offender are also based on learned responses to family sexual abuse. People in the offender role have been sexually abused. Their response to that abuse is a persistent pattern of sexual victimization of others to avoid their own pain. People in the denier role have lived with ongoing sexual abuse in their family-of-origin, and they have often been sexually abused as well. They learn to respond to the abuse of others and/or their own abuse by denying the reality of the abuse.

Nearly all of you reading this book were in the victim role in your families, because offenders and deniers are not very interested in recovery. Family members in the denier and offender roles get the most out of the system as it is, while you, like others in the victim role, get the least out of the system. You are reading this because you are struggling to move beyond the helpless role of victim to the empowered status of survivor.

The Offender

The offender is a person who has been sexually abused. Offenders may deny any history of sexual abuse, but they are likely to either have repressed memories or to lie about their own abuse. They protect and defend other offenders, including those who abused them.

Offenders learned as young children to deal with their own sexual abuse by identifying with the aggressor and taking out on others any negative feelings they have. During the offender's abuse as a child, the focus was on the abuser. "Only the strong survive," their thinking goes. "Better to be one of the strong than one of the weak. Better to be the one who does the hurting than the one who gets hurt."

They sexually abuse for a wide variety of reasons, but the central motivation is to stop any emerging feelings or memories about their own childhood sexual abuse. This triggers the rule they live by: Take it out on someone else. The act of sexual abuse proves that they are in control and no longer in danger of being hurt. Much of what they do to others is precisely what was done to them.

Most offenders are sexually compulsive. They have sex frequently, in a variety of ways, and with a variety of people, objects, and oftentimes animals. One of the common myths about incest is that the father or stepfather turns to his daughter because his sexual needs are not being met by his cold, unappealing wife. This is no more true than believing that alcoholics drink because they're thirsty.

Offenders are excited by pornography, sexual fantasizing, affairs, wife rape, child abuse, compulsive masturbation, or any other sexual activity they can dream up. Individuals have their "sex of choice," like drug addicts have their "drug of choice." If their preferred activity is not available, most anything or anyone will do.

More males fill the offender role than females. We know that the hormone testosterone increases sex drive, so there may well be a physiological component to sexual compulsivity. Another factor is intricately bound up in the sexism that exists in our culture. The expectations of the societally defined role for males grooms them more so than females for the controlling, dominating, sexually focused offender role.

Regardless of gender, certain characteristics are necessary for those in the offender role. If children have these characteristics, they will take on the offender role in their families. If they do not have these characteristics, they will fulfill one of the other two roles.

Those in the offender role must have a high need for control and well-developed rationalization skills. They need to be good at projecting their feelings onto others instead of feeling emotions themselves. They must be able to block out others' pain, and self-centeredness is an absolute necessity.

Above all, offenders must lack the capacity for remorse or guilt. So many survivors hope desperately that their perpetrators will feel anguish at the destruction they wrought. If offenders could feel anguish and compassion for others, they would not have been able to abuse a child in the first place.

The Denier

As children, all deniers must cope with living in a family where brothers and sisters are being molested or raped. They soon grasp that the requirement of survival in the covert family system is to ignore all signs of abuse. If mom is sleeping with your kid brother, pay no attention. If you see dad touching sister's breast, close your eyes. It is no wonder that, as adults, deniers are found in marriages where they are oblivious to the abuse going on around them.

Deniers believe that the best way to survive is to ingratiate themselves with the offenders in the family and keep a low profile. They know who has the power in the family, and they work diligently to stay on the good side of the offender. When they themselves are sexually abused, they deal with it by minimizing the abuse and then forgetting about it as soon as possible. They mistakenly assume that their fawning acceptance of the offender is the reason offenders do not target them for as much abuse as those in the victim role.

Deniers are masters of offering trite phrases in response to pain. "Don't dwell on it," "Let bygones be bygones," "Forgive and forget," and "You can't change the past" are common platitudes deniers deliver when confronted with sexual abuse. These banalities are always directed at the victim, of course, whether the victim is their brother, sister, or their own child.

Their responses to abuse are offender-oriented, that is, designed to protect and defend the offender. A great deal of variation exists in the aggressiveness of deniers in protecting the offender, however. Some are completely self-involved and ignorant of the ongoing abuse. Their response to disclosure of abuse shows a lack of compassion for their children or their siblings and a selfish focus on their own lives.

Martha's mother was a classic example of this type

of denial. When she heard that Martha had been raped by her father for the last ten years, she sobbed, "What am I going to do? This will ruin my job, and we'll be outcasts in the town. And who's going to take care of your father now? You know what an animal he is."

Other deniers viciously attack the victim and protect the offender. They are belligerent or even assault those in the victim role. "You lying slut!" one mother screamed at her ten-year-old daughter when the little girl blurted out that her father had molested her. "You've always been more trouble than you're worth. You should have been drowned at birth."

The Victim

The person in the victim role is the target for much of the offender's sexual abuse. Other children in the family are probably sexually abused also, but the child in the victim role has certain qualities that mark him or her for "special attention" from the perpetrator. Thus, victims are usually more systematically and severely abused than their siblings.

Victims are often the best and the brightest the family has to offer. Their role demands enormous strength and adaptability. Offenders want to destroy anything they cannot have, and the strength and vitality of the victims simultaneously attracts and enrages them. Victims become the recipients of punishing, pervasive abuse from offenders, so they must be strong.

In addition to being terribly sexually abused, they are objects of role reversal. In role reversal, the child becomes the adult, and the parent becomes the child. Victims are expected to take care of their parents, along with other children in the family. They must be strong enough to survive the onslaught of abuse and neglect they receive while still providing the responsible nurturing required of them as surrogate parents.

Besides being strong and intelligent, children in the victim role are selected because they are very sensitive. Sensitivity is a very appealing quality to offenders, who have a tremendous need to see someone else suffer. A sensitive, feeling child is the perfect foil for a callous offender bent on seeing his or her own pain reflected on another's face.

Victims are criticized by both offenders and deniers for being sensitive. "You're too sensitive," they are told over and over by those whose reality depends on being insensitive. Most adults who have been in the victim role cringe when anyone tells them they are sensitive. In fact, sensitivity is a lovely trait, and one to be cherished in any human being.

Victims take on others' feelings and incorporate them into their own being, including whatever feelings the offender is denying. During an act of sexual abuse, guilt, rage, and shame are dumped by the offender and absorbed by the vulnerable victim. The offender is relieved, while the victim feels guilty, rageful, and ashamed.

Children in the victim role sometimes act out their abuse on younger children, but this does not mean they are offenders. They are children doing what they learn to do, and they do not continue as adults with a persistent pattern of sexual victimization to avoid their own pain. They also feel a great deal of remorse and guilt for their actions. Victims' responses to sexually exploiting someone else are diametrically opposed to offenders' responses.

THE WALTONS REVISITED

Below is a sample chart showing an incest family according to roles, whom we shall call the Waltons. The O is for offender, D for denier, and V is for victim. The

Family Chart

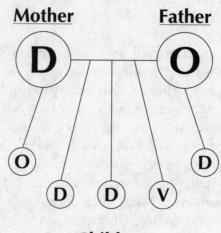

Children

chart represents a typical incest family, but many variations exist on how the offender, denier, and victim roles are dispersed in families.

The Waltons are a classic incest family, with the father in the offender role and the mother in the denier role. In other families, though, the mother may be in the offender role while the father is a denier, in some both parents are deniers with siblings in the offender role, and so on. In severely abusive families, both parents are offenders, and the damage this system wreaks is often lethal.

As is usually the case, only one child is in the victim role in this family. Sexually abusive families cannot afford to have more than one child in the victim role per nuclear family, because alliances among victims would be too threatening to the existence of the abusive system. The siblings are all either deniers or offenders. The

Extended Family Chart

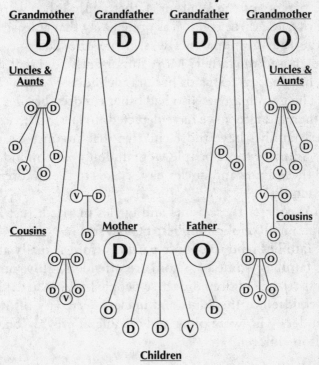

Grandmother (D)   **Grandfather** (D)   **Grandfather** (D)   **Grandmother** (O)

Uncles & Aunts

Uncles & Aunts

Cousins

Cousins

Mother (D)   **Father** (O)

Children

victim is outnumbered, and any attempt to deal with the sexual abuse will be met with silencing, punishing responses by the other family members.

The Extended Family

Sexual abuse is always intergenerational, and every one in a sexually abusive system takes one of these roles. The parents of the Waltons' father and mother were in one of these three roles. It is quite likely that at least one of the four grandparents was in the offender role, for who abused the father? More importantly, did that person have access to his or her grandchildren?

The grandparents also had other children besides the mother and father we have depicted. In fact, statistically incest families have more children than nonincest families. Some of these people were undoubtedly offenders. Did these aunts and uncles have access to the children in this family?

Of course, these aunts and uncles married. Just like people in alcoholic families, people from sexually abusive families tend to choose partners from sexually abusive families, some of whom are offenders. How much access to the children did these people have? What about the children of the aunts and uncles? Were any of them offenders who were older and capable of preying on the Walton children?

The Family Network of Offenders

Adult survivors leaving a one-month outpatient treatment center for sexual abuse reported having an average of *seven* offenders! It is no small wonder when we look at the extended family chart. The number of potential abusers is shocking. Victims are growing up in family networks riddled with offenders who are protected by a cadre of deniers.

To complicate the situation even more, offenders and deniers also choose other offenders and deniers for friends. They pick these people through an unconscious awareness of shared values and interests. Doctors, ministers, babysitters, and others who have access to the children often come from sexually abusive systems.

Ellen, whose father was a blatantly crude offender, once described her first meeting with a man who later raped her for several years. "He came over to ask to borrow some farm equipment and brought his kids along. When his oldest daughter came in, he made a joke about her breasts being really sexy, and my dad laughed.

"Then my dad pinched my sister's butt when she went by. They both thought this was hilarious. My dad kicked my three-year-old brother really hard when he started to whine. It was like he was telling him he could do whatever he wanted to us kids because we weren't anything. The guy left, and you could tell each thought the other one was just great."

The Network of Offenders and Memory Repression

Multiple abusers increase the likelihood of memory repression. The sheer number of abusers becomes overwhelming. When overload is reached, or if a particular perpetrator is bizarre or brutal, memory repression is used as a survival tool. It reduces the number of remembered abusers and incidents to a manageable level.

The odds that a child will be abused before he or she is old enough to remember are also very high. With the web of available offenders in any sexually abusive system, at least one of these offenders is likely not to care how young a child is, and some may actually prefer babies and toddlers for their sexual objects. Chances are slim in a sexually abusive family system that a child will get past the age of five without being abused.

EMPOWERING YOURSELF

Is the covert system in your family more disturbed than you thought possible for such a "normal" family as yours? Make a list of your nuclear and extended family members by name. After each name, list any problem or dysfunction you know of or suspect. Include things like depression, alcohol or drug abuse, troubled marriages, living at home past an acceptable age of emancipation, and behaviors indicating sexual compulsivity and victimization. Err on the side of overstating problems, rather than on the side of denial.

Using the family chart as a model, on a large piece of paper or tagboard, put the names of your nuclear family members and signify their role and yours using O for offender, D for denier, and V for victim. You may want to expand the chart to include your extended family members, too.

A word of caution is necessary, however. In abusive families, children are raised to feel sorry for their parents, especially their mothers. Do not let your awareness of your parents' pain influence you into deciding that one of them is in the victim role. Decide what role they have on the basis of their response to your sexual abuse, not on sympathy for their suffering.

CHAPTER FIVE

MEMORY RECOVERY WORK

Sarah's suspicions about her grandfather surfaced one day in therapy when she blurted out, "I'm pretty sure my grandpa did sexual stuff to me. A family story from my babyhood is that my mom found me crawling away from him through cutweeds. Cutweeds have really sharp edges, and my hands and knees were supposedly pretty badly scratched. Why would a little baby crawl through cutweeds unless she were scared?"

The next week I brought up her statement about her grandfather's abuse. "I don't know why I said such a thing. I don't remember if my crawling away from my grandpa was part of the family story. I didn't even know I was going to say that he may have abused me until the words were out of my mouth." Looking shamefaced, she said, "I think I just made that up to get attention."

Sarah also reported that she kept flashing on images of a body hanging by one arm and hitting the side of a building. "It bothers me a lot," she cried. "I'm not scared of the picture in my mind or anything like that. It just keeps popping up, over and over again. I don't have any memories that fit anything like this, either. I must be really nuts."

Sarah did have memories that fit with the image and the words she blurted out. The words she spoke about her grandfather and the persistent imagery of the body slamming into a wall were memory fragments, not manifestations of craziness or symbolic representations of her abuse. Her memories were inside her, recorded and stored in the filing system in her brain. They only needed to be accessed.

Human beings have five kinds of memory. The mind has a process for recording, storing, and retrieving everything that happens by using at least one of these memory processes. Understanding how all these forms of memory work will help you retrieve your repressed memories.

THE FIVE KINDS OF MEMORY

Both the conscious and the unconscious have the capability to record and access events and information. Recall memory is the memory process for the conscious mind. Imagistic memory, feeling memory, body memory, and acting-out memory are the memory processes of the unconscious mind. Survivors and therapists are beginning to explore the capabilities of these forms of memory together.

Recall Memory

Recall memory is a consciously retained memory of events accompanied by the sense of having experienced those events. It involves a series of related images organized around time and space into a logical sequence. For example, if we are asked to recall last year's Christmas, a series of thoughts, feelings, and images is available mentally.

We trust recall memory because our brain sends recognition signals that tell us, "This really happened to me." The recognition signals are a flood of related associations to the events we are trying to remember.

Unlike the other four kinds of memory, we are not disassociated from the feelings and related stimuli around the events we are picturing.

Recall memory is the only form of memory that requires maturation to be of use. Infants of a few days have virtually no recall abilities at first. They are soon able to recognize their parents, and their recall abilities grow rapidly. Two-year-olds have much more recall capability, but compared to adults they are still quite limited.

The unconscious records memories that the conscious mind is incapable of storing. Abuse that happens to us before our recall memories are fully developed and abuse that is extremely traumatic are stored in the unconscious. These memories must be accessed using the unconscious forms of memory.

Imagistic Memory

Imagistic memory is a memory that breaks through to the conscious mind in the form of imagery. This imagery is actually an incomplete picture of events that happened. The images are like a slide show. They pop up and are gone in an instant, often leaving the person wondering, "Now where did *that* come from?"

A study by the U.S. Army suggests that imagery reflects real aspects of a trauma. After the Gander military disaster, in which an Army plane crashed in Gander, Newfoundland, killing all on board, a study was done of those who assisted at the disaster scene. The Army personnel who had retrieved, identified, and bagged bodies were found to be suffering some PTSD symptoms, and one of the more common post-trauma reactions was seeing intrusive flashes related to the disaster.

What the soldiers flashed on varied greatly, but whatever they saw was directly related to the work they did at the accident site. That is, those who matched limbs to torsos saw limbless people, those who made identifications by dental X-rays saw jawbones and skulls, and those who bagged bodies saw lumps of burned flesh. Each image related concretely and specifically to the grisly work of the person experiencing it.

As we can see from the soldiers' experiences at the Gander tragedy, imagistic memory can be activated by trauma. The trauma of abuse is not something the mind or body forgets. If the memory is not stored in the conscious mind, it will be stored in the unconscious. Sooner or later, that memory will emerge, often in the form of imagistic memory.

When the images from repressed memories do come spilling out, they are persistent and uniquely compelling. The same image occurs repeatedly, sometimes three times, sometimes hundreds of times over years. However many times the same image flashes, it seems to stick in your mind, as if your psyche has underlined it with invisible ink. Sarah, like the rest of us, probably has numerous random thoughts and pictures floating throughout her consciousness. The image of a body slamming into a wall caught her attention by its persistence and her intuitive sense that it was of special significance.

Images that surface from the unconscious can be from any part of the abuse scene. They may be weapons or objects used in sexual abuse, or body parts, especially penises and vaginas. Bizarre flashes of violence, such as a child hanging by a rope or blood squirting from a severed hand, can emerge because this part of the abuse was so traumatic to the child. It is also quite common that the images are of seemingly neutral scenes that the child focused on during the abuse, like a bedroom door or a flash of a man's shirt.

Some aspects of the imagery may be exaggerated, even though each image represents an accurate slice of the abuse. The image of a severed hand squirting blood may, in reality, be a hand that has been cut and bleeding profusely, not severed. Images may also appear stylized, as if they are cartoonlike or plastic. These differences between the imagery and the reality of the abuse are the result of the impact of massive anxiety on perception. The child undergoing shocking trauma is so flooded with fear and apprehension that what is happening may seem magnified or unreal.

The most confusing thing about the images is that they seem unrelated to what is happening at the present moment. They are, in fact, triggered by something in the environment that reminds their unconscious of the buried memory. The associated memory breaks through the unconscious as an image.

For over a year, Janet had been dealing with her brother's sexual abuse of her when she began to have persistent images of knives whenever she was driving. At first they were single images of long butcher knives. Then blips of knives being inserted in a stomach or a vagina began to intrude on her thoughts. She was frightened and mystified, for she had no physical history or scars that fit with her being cut with a knife. Her brother's abuse of her seemed to be characterized by opportunistic fondling, not violent, threatening assaults. And why did these images flash when she was driving?

Janet's imagery gradually revealed a story of nightmare abuse by a trusted family friend. He abused Janet sexually whenever she was left in the care of his wife for the three years he lived next door to Janet. On several occasions he took Janet to the local Dairy Queen, stopping the car in the park on the way to abuse and terrify her. One of his favorite "turn-ons" was to use a knife as an erotic object, running it over her and carefully inserting the tip in or near her vagina.

Janet's mystery was solved. The knife imagery was not symbolic of her rage at her brother's molestation, as she had first suspected. It was a memory surfacing in a disassociated fashion, a freeze-frame picture of a portion of her forgotten abuse by this man. She said, "The first time I saw the image of the knife, I was driving to get myself a treat. Now I know why it happened then. It makes so much sense!"

Feeling Memory

The emotional system is part of the memory process of our minds. When we recall our last birthday, we often have an emotional reaction associated with our recall. We may feel sad or lonely if our birthday was a painful one, or we may feel a flood of happiness as we remember last year's outpouring of gifts and support.

Feeling memory is the memory of an emotional response to a particular situation. If the situation we are being triggered to remember is a repressed memory, we will have the feelings pertaining to the event without any conscious recall of the event itself. Feeling memory is often experienced as a flood of inexplicable emotion, particularly around abuse issues.

A felt sense that something abusive has happened is a common form of a feeling memory. Some survivors will say, "Yes, I think I was sexually abused, but it's just a gut feeling." These clients are experiencing a feeling memory about being abused, even though at that moment they can recall nothing about their abuse.

Rose felt frightened and angry whenever she became ill even with a mild cold or headache. Memory recovery work revealed that her grandfather, who was a physician and a sexual sadist, was always called to treat her when she was sick as a child. He would abuse her hideously in the course of his examination and treatment. As an adult, Rose would be triggered by any illness into a feeling memory of her grandfather's abuse without knowing why.

Feeling memory often occurs in combination with

other forms of memory. An apparently neutral image may be accompanied by a wave of sadness or fear, or genital pain can be linked with a deep sense of shame. Many survivors retrieving memories through imagistic work or dream analysis have feeling memories as they progress through a series of images, validating their sense of reality about what they are remembering.

Body Memory

Our bodies react to everything that happens to us, and body memory is the physical manifestation of a past incident. The more significant the incident is, the greater the impact on the body. Our physical bodies always remember sexual abuse, just as our feelings and our minds do.

Jim was a survivor who had been sexually abused by his mother. He was rightfully very angry at his father for ignoring his distress signals and giving covert permission for the abuse. Whenever he talked about his anger at his father, however, he reported that his anus hurt. At first he passed this off as a random pain spasm, then thought of it as an idiosyncratic physical reaction to anger. When he began to work on dreams and imagery around the possibility of his father sexually abusing him, the pain intensified dramatically. His body was remembering the pain of his father's anal rapes.

Even when there is little physical pain or intrusion, body memories can occur. Nausea is a frequent physical reaction to sexual abuse. Infants will sometimes spontaneously vomit on their perpetrator, even though they are not being physically hurt by the abuse. Genital awareness or arousal are other common body memories of sexual abuse that is not physically violent.

Like imagistic and feeling memory, body memory often emerges in conjunction with other forms of unconscious memory processes. Survivors' legs shake as they remember the physical strain of uncomfortable sexual positions, genitals hurt as feelings surface, or an arm aches after a dream of being turned over for sexual access by being pulled by the arm. The body memories, alone or with other forms of memory, tell the story of the sexual abuse.

Acting-out Memory

Acting-out memory is a form of unconscious memory in which the forgotten incident is spontaneously acted out through some physical action. It involves either a verbal or bodily act in response to something that reminds one of the original episode. When Sarah blurted out that she thought her grandfather had abused her, and later said she had no idea why she said that, she was experiencing acting-out memory.

A two-year-old who was developmentally delayed had been adopted at the age of three months after having been physically abused. Whenever this little child was angry, she would smack herself on the left ear. Her mother explained to her play therapist, "One thing we know for sure from her medical history is that she was burned on her left ear with a cigarette when she was two months old. She's hit herself on her left ear ever since we got her." As the toddler worked through her feelings of tremendous fear and anger, she gradually dropped the self-injuring behavior.

Perhaps the most common kind of acting-out memory is when survivors suddenly say something about their abuse that they had no intention of saying. Doug told his therapy group about a memory he had of seeing his mother lying on her bed, bleeding vaginally. He said he then had to clean her up and put a sanitary pad on her. When group members brought up the issue the following week, he seemed chagrined.

"That never happened," he said. "I just said that and I have no idea why." The issue was dropped, but several months later Doug reported that he now believed he said it because it really had happened. "Now I have the pictures and the feelings that go with that scene. It was like the words were the first memory I had of it."

Physically acting out part of an abuse memory is another manifestation of this kind of memory. Gary recovered memories of his mother forcing him to have oral sex with her in infancy and early childhood. After he remembered this abuse, he recounted his first adolescent sexual experience. "I was in the back seat of the car with my date at a drive-in movie. Suddenly she leaned over and kissed me on the mouth. The next thing I knew I was on the floor of the car on my knees with my head in her lap. I was horribly embarrassed and confused. I had no idea of why I did that. Now I know."

Acting-out memory can occur even when you are asleep. A dream may contain a fragment of an abuse memory, triggering an acting-out memory. Survivors have awoken from sleep finding themselves cowering under the bed or running down the hall yelling, "Stay away from me." Similar reactions can also occur under the influence of drugs and alcohol.

SPONTANEOUS RECALL OF ABUSE MEMORIES

Sometimes buried memories of abuse emerge spontaneously. A triggering event or catalyst starts the memories flowing. The survivor then experiences the memories as a barrage of images about the abuse and related details. Memories that are retrieved in this manner are relatively easy to understand and believe because the person remembering is so flooded with coherent, consistent information.

If an abuse memory does not materialize spontaneously, it rarely surfaces as a recall memory. The memory instead returns through the unconscious memory processes. Survivors will have a series of realizations about their abuse that they find clear and believable, but rarely do they have a sense of having lived what is being felt or pictured. They call it a memory because the pieces fit into their sense of reality, not because they actually now remember experiencing the abuse.

What most people call spontaneous recall usually involves memories that have been denied, not repressed. The survivor has always been aware that the sexual abuse happened, but he or she has studiously avoided thinking about it. A catalyst sets the memory process in motion, but the essential factor in the memory surfacing is the readiness of the survivor to deal with the reality of the abuse.

Joan was a college student in therapy dealing with codependency and emotional abuse in her family-of-origin. During spring break her parents asked her to house sit for them while they went to Europe, and Joan agreed. While they were gone, Joan got in touch with an abuse memory.

"I suddenly remembered the other time my parents' went to Europe. I was eight, and they left me with a neighbor. One night the neighborhood kids were all playing hide-and-seek. I hid in the bushes in the yard of this really old couple. The old woman came out of the house and found me. She told me to come in the house, and there she showed me this candy bar I could have if I went down the basement with her husband."

Joan began sobbing. "I felt like I was supposed to do whatever grown-ups told me, and I really wanted that candy bar, so I went with him. He stuck his penis in my mouth. I hated it. Then I got the candy bar and went outside with the other kids. When they asked me where I got the candy bar, I threw it away. I was so ashamed."

Joan had always known this happened to her, but she put the memory away and never thought about it. Prompted by her prior work in therapy and the similarity in circumstance of her parents' leaving her to go to Europe, the memory abruptly became three-dimensional. As Joan recalled the incident, it took on the appropriate meaning and significance for the first time.

MEMORY RETRIEVAL TECHNIQUES

Few survivors experience spontaneous recall, especially if they have no awareness of the abuse ever happening. Most are forced to endure months or years of fear, confusion, and doubt as their memories surface. Dreams, imagery, feelings, and physical symptoms must be painstakingly faced and pieced together into a meaningful whole that the survivor struggles to accept as reality.

Currently, seven major methods of memory retrieval are being used for retrieving memories. Once you become familiar with them, you can focus on the memory recovery techniques that most fit your needs. Please seek out an experienced therapist to help you with this work. You do not have to go through this process alone.

Imagistic work. Imagistic work relies on the use of imagistic memory to retrieve abuse memories buried in the unconscious. Some guidance is given by a therapist or other supportive person to expand on or explore images that have broken through to the conscious mind, allowing related images of the abuse to surface. The process lets the survivor complete the picture of what happened, using a current image or flash as a jumping-off point. A detailed description of how to do imagistic work is given in Chapter Six.

Dream work. Repressed memories often surface through our dreams, when the boundary between the unconscious and conscious mind is permeable. Images float through our dreams that capture our attention. After we awaken we can expand on the images and sensations evoked by our dreams to shed light on or recover our repressed memories. Chapter Seven will give useful guidelines on using dream work to retrieve memories.

Journal writing. Writing, especially spontaneous, free-association writing, can often tap into buried memories. Survivors can utilize acting-out memory through this form of journal writing, using either images they have or structured exercises as a starting point. Guidelines for the use of journal writing to retrieve memories appear in Chapter Eight.

Body work. Massage therapy or body manipulation techniques access body memories for survivors. As certain places on the body are touched or certain movements are made, memories of abuse may surface through any of the five kinds of memory. Body work is often used by survivors to aid in memory work, and it will also be discussed in Chapter Eight.

Hypnosis. When a trance state is induced by a qualified hypnotist, hypnosis can often be used to retrieve buried memories. This involves tapping into the unconscious via imagistic memory. Chapter Eight will discuss the pros and cons of hypnosis as a technique, as well as the importance of finding a qualified and ethical hypnotist.

Feelings work. Reexperiencing the feelings of great rage or terror or abandonment may trigger the memory related to the feelings to surface. The feelings work is usually best done in a structured setting with a therapist present to guide the work and serve as a reality contact.

Chapter Eight gives more information on the use of feelings work.

Art therapy. Art therapy involves the use of the creative process to surface feelings and memories. Either the survivor re-creates a portion of the memory in the artwork, or the completed work acts as a trigger for the recovery of a repressed memory. Art therapy can be used as the major source of memory recovery or as an adjunct to other forms of recall. We will examine art therapy more closely in Chapter Eight.

GENERAL GUIDELINES FOR MEMORY WORK

You never get repressed memories back by trying to remember them. If your memories are to surface, you must look for them by piecing together clues from your past, your feelings, your dreams and images, and your body. You can help your memories surface, but you cannot make them surface. Sitting down in a chair and concentrating on your childhood, trying to remember, will only access what you already know.

Going over what you already know about your childhood can be helpful in clearing the field, so to speak, for the repressed memories to surface. Memories can be blocked by unfinished or shallow debriefing of known abuse, but working on those memories only prepares the path. It does not guarantee that whatever is forgotten will automatically emerge.

Repressed memories also never feel the same as recall memories. You will not have the sense of having experienced the abuse you are remembering. Expect your repressed memories to have a hazy, dissociated quality to them, even after working with them over an extended period of time. You will gradually come to know that they are real, but not in the same way you remember something that was never repressed.

You must learn to weave together all five kinds of memory to discover what happened to you. Body memories, feeling memories, acting-out memories, or imagistic memories rarely emerge in isolation. Instead of a single memory fragment surfacing, you may develop a headache accompanied by an image of a child crying, followed by a strange dream about oral sex that leaves you feeling bruised and bereft. You may also obsess on some trivial recall memory from your childhood, like losing your jacket at the third-grade picnic. These forms of memory are presenting information to you about a single abusive incident that happened after your picnic, leaving you with an aching head and a sense of abandonment.

With your current therapist or professionals, explain clearly why you think you have repressed memories. Ask professionals how much experience they have in this area and how they generally proceed in retrieving repressed memories. Then share your ideas on how you want to approach your repressed memories. Talk over anything that feels unsafe or confusing.

If a therapist states that it is harmful to retrieve or clarify repressed memories, you may want to explore why he or she believes this. Be aware that some therapists take this approach because they do not have the necessary skills or experience in working with repressed memories, while, for others, potential harm is a legitimate concern. If a therapist does caution you against working on your memories, and this does not fit with your own sense of what you need to do, seek a second or third opinion.

Some of you may need to be quite cautious in uncovering your repressed memories. If you are prone to flashbacks, in which you relive the abusive incident, you may need the safeguard of a hospital setting when your memories surface. If retrieving your repressed memories activates a suicidal depression, or in any other way seriously endangers your well-being, you need to postpone the work until you have achieved a greater sense of stability.

You can expect dry spells and backsliding to happen. Months may go by when you have little or no interest in your repressed memories. They become some weird fantasy that bears no relationship to your present life. Often this happens after contact with your family-of-origin, which has a huge investment in your memories staying unreal. Wait out these periods, for they inevitably pass. Use the time to work on what you do recall, or on problems in the here and now.

Let your pain be your guide. Focus on your repressed memories for at least one year. If you feel healthier after that period of time, you are on the right track. You may have periods of disbelief, but suspend a final judgment until enough time has elapsed to see if healing has occurred for you. Remember, you are going on a journey. You will know when you are at your destination.

EMPOWERING YOURSELF

Use the following list to help you start to sort out any memories that may be emerging. At first you may have very little to put on the list, but this will change over time. It is helpful to keep updating your list as new memory pieces emerge. Share your list with your therapist, and talk over how you want to approach memory work.

Imagistic memories. List any persistent, unusual, or troublesome images you have had recently or in your past. Include images from dreams or sleep states.

Feeling memories. List any strong emotional sensations you have had related to abuse, or any unusual feelings you have that do not seem attached to your present life.

Body memories. List any bothersome or painful body sensations you have had. Include any information you know about when these sensations happen or what they suggest about what might have happened to your body.

Acting-out memory. List your odd or surprising actions or words you have blurted out without knowing why. Also list any actions or words that you felt like doing or saying but did not.

Your own list. Jot down suspected memories of abuse you would like to explore. Include your own felt sense of how you think you were abused, or any other information that is important to you.

CHAPTER SIX

IMAGISTIC WORK

Sarah came in for her therapy session very distraught. "I was presenting a budget to the board of directors when I got that flash of a body slamming into a wall that I've been seeing lately. Only this time it scared me. I started shaking and I lost my train of thought. I think it's a memory, and I want to know what it's about!"

We discussed several options for exploring what she now believed to be a memory fragment. Since the memory was arising as an image, she decided to try imagistic work. She closed her eyes and related everything she could see or sense about the image, leaving out no detail, no matter how small. I encouraged her to add her own interpretations about the image.

"I see a body. I think of a child, swinging down toward a wall. My sense is that the body is suspended by one arm. It swings down and hits the wall or side of the structure. I think someone is holding the child by one arm. I can vaguely see a rough wooden wall with a strut or support coming down at a right angle next to where the child hits. Or maybe she hits the strut and not the wall. And I do think it's a girl—actually, I think it's me, like at two or so years old."

Sarah was quiet for several seconds. She seemed very focused on her internal reality. With a disgusted look on her face, she said, "I can smell an outdoor toilet. I'm scared that maybe I am going to be dropped. I keep flashing on my grandfather.

"I think my grandfather is lowering me down the toilet hole in the outhouse behind his house. I get the sense that he's spaced out, like he's just doing it to see how I will react. My arm hurts, and I keep twisting slightly as he holds onto my wrist and lets me hang."

I asked her to let herself picture the beginning of this memory. "I see my grandpa taking me by the hand and leading me into the outhouse. He closes and latches the door. I don't want him to do that.

"He sits down, pulls his pants down, and takes out his penis. Then he puts me on his lap and pulls my underpants down. I'm wearing a blue dress. He starts to rub his penis between my legs." She paused. "But I feel like I'm just making this up!"

I urged her to continue, explaining that truth or fantasy is not of concern at the beginning of memory retrieval work. What is important is what was in her mind and what seemed true at this moment in time. She continued, "He squirts stuff on me from his penis. Then he laughs a funny little laugh. He tells me no one cares about me, I'm just garbage. Then he lowers me into the toilet hole of the outhouse. I try to hang on his arm, but I'm only two or three years old and I'm not strong enough. I swing from his arm and hit that beam on the side. The smell is awful. I'm really scared."

By now, Sarah was white-faced. Her hands were shaking, and she began to cry quietly. After resting a moment, she finished the scene. In a voice barely above a whisper, she continued. "He finally pulls me out. I'm crying and he tells me to shut up and gives me a little shake. He wipes my face and pulls up my pants. He opens the door, and we go into the yard. He goes into the house, but I stay outside. I'm surprised at how sunny and pretty the world looks. Somehow it seems as if it should be all dark and gloomy."

Sarah had completed the process of imagistic retrieval of an abuse memory. She tapped into imagistic memory from her unconscious, and then reported what her mind and body suggested to her about the possible sequence of events of this abuse incident. The memory that had been stalking Sarah's life was finally fully exposed.

At the end of her work, Sarah was in a state of shock. She sensed that the feelings would set in later, and she needed reassurance that she would not be overwhelmed. I assured her that the traumatized child has many creative ways of buffering pain, so that survivors are seldom faced with more than they can handle. After retrieving a memory, aftershocks of the emotional detonations usually happen in waves. Although the waves would get stronger and then recede, no single wave would overpower her, and she had a strong support network to rely on in the days to come.

In spite of her distress, Sarah knew that the benefits of retrieving this memory outweighed the costs. She immediately felt less apprehensive about the symptoms that preceded the emergence of this memory. Behaviors that at first seemed bizarre now clearly seemed manifestations of damage from the abuse.

"Finally I know why I get so panicked in bathrooms and why I can't close bathroom doors," Sarah said. "And the image of a body swinging by one arm makes more sense. If I see it again, at least I'll know what it means."

Her terrifying panic attacks would also improve. Panic attacks often serve as the unconscious's early warning system for repressed memories. The uncon-

scious is trying to signal the mind and body of the survivor that a trauma is about to be reexperienced. Now
that Sarah consciously acknowledged the existence of
the memory, the panic attacks would very likely subside
as she became involved with other feelings about the
abuse.

GUIDED IMAGISTIC WORK

The images that surface from your unconscious to
your conscious mind are fragments of a traumatic memory ready to emerge. These blips flashing across your
mind may be mystifying or obscure at first glance, but
they are an incomplete scrap from an abuse incident that
you have buried. A piece of that incident has broken
through and is poking into your conscious mind. Follow it down into your unconscious and you will retrieve
a repressed memory.

Some of you get an image and seem to experience
almost instant awareness of its true significance in your
personal history. You simply need permission to acknowledge and talk about your memories. You have a
unique ability to reclaim all you need to know from
your unconscious with a sense of certainty and release.

For others, tapping into imagistic memory involves
uncertainty, blank spots, and slowly unfolding revela-
tions about the abuse long after their first awareness of
a memory fragment. You can tap into your imagistic
memory, but you need a method and a guide to help
you.

The following is a map to guide you in your process.
You and your therapist may already be doing a version
of this work. Many therapists who are experienced in
working with abuse issues use this method, although
they may have different labels for the basic processes. If

you have not done some form of imagistic memory retrieval in your therapy, bring up your interest in the method to your therapist and discuss the possibility of doing this work in your sessions.

If you do not have a therapist who does this kind of work to act as your guide, you can use a close friend or support person, provided you feel strong enough and safe enough with them to explore your memories outside of therapy. Be sure to check with your therapist before you do this work outside of therapy, however. He or she can help you assess your physical and emotional safety in doing this memory work.

You may need to adjust the method to the style of the person who guides you, but an outside person is essential to the process. Doing the work by yourself would require you to play a dual role. You would need to ask yourself the necessary questions to elicit associated images and simultaneously observe images and other reactions. With a guide, you can concentrate solely on how your mind and body are responding to the process.

If your guide is not familiar with guided imagistic work, you can suggest reading this chapter. Both of you should then discuss your expectations about doing this work. If either of you feel uncomfortable proceeding, it is best not to go ahead. You may need to select someone else as your guide or choose an alternative method of memory retrieval.

It is important to remember that retrieving repressed memories is never an orderly, logical process. When you access your imagistic memory, other kinds of memory are stimulated also. Images are interspersed with feelings, body memories, and urges to say or act out what happened to you. All of these pieces must be woven together to arrive at a coherent sense of your abuse.

Selecting a Focal Point

First you must have a focal point to begin imagistic work. The focal point used to begin drawing on imagistic memory can be anything that seems to contain a reference to a repressed memory of abuse. A repetitive, compelling image that has some element or feel of abuse is the most logical focal point, but imagistic memory can be tapped using other focal points as well. You can focus on a dream fragment, a feeling, a body sensation, an object that seems frightening, or a phrase that is stuck in your mind.

If you have several possible focal points, selecting one to work on can be problematic. If one of the possibilities seems to be either more disturbing or prominent for you, work with that one. If not, you may want to start with the focal point that seems to be the most explicitly related to sexual abuse or the one in which the client seems to be the youngest.

Kelly was a lovely dark-haired woman who suffered from debilitating shyness and a crippling sense of shame. She had made wonderful strides in group therapy working on her physical abuse history and self-esteem. When she began to get flashes of possible sexual abuse by her mother, she was eager to probe more deeply into her memories, through imagistic work.

Kelly described three images that had been intruding into her consciousness recently. "One is an image of being in the bathtub with my mother when I was very young, maybe one or two. The other is of a huge breast thrust at me, really mashed against my face. I also have a picture of my hand being pulled toward a woman's crotch. I don't know where to start."

None of the three memory fragments elicited a strong emotional reaction. She felt numb and was not having any feelings. Nor did she sense any sort of draw or pull toward one of them. Then a group member asked her in which of the three she thought she was the youngest. She teared up and said, "I get the sense that when my hand was pulled toward the crotch, it was a really tiny hand." That memory fragment became Kelly's focal point.

Preparation

Imagistic memory work uses the focal point to try to string together a sequence of events that will form a complete memory. Whether what is remembered around that focal point is made up or real is of no concern at the beginning of the process; that can be decided at a later date. You need only to see what images are in your mind about the focal point, along with any related body or feeling memories.

Seat yourself comfortably and take a few relaxing breaths before you begin the actual work. Most people prefer doing imagistic work with their eyes closed. Outside stimulation is kept to a minimum, and you can focus all your attention on your internal reality. Closing your eyes is not a necessity, however, if you are frightened or feel you can work better with your eyes open.

Whoever is guiding the memory will ask questions to help you picture or sense what is happening in relation to that focal point. If nothing surfaces, wait a bit, and then give your best guess in answer to the questions. If you feel resistance or skepticism, try to go past it. If you cannot, then stop and discuss it with your guide before moving on.

It is important to monitor your internal reactions very carefully. You may get an image, a feeling, or just a vague sense of something you want to say in response to a question. Share all of your reactions; really listen to yourself and verbalize whatever comes up.

The most important instruction is *do not censor*. Images, urges, and reactions must be observed carefully and reported as accurately as possible. At times the desire to censor or judge what is seen or felt may be strong, but be as honest as it is possible to be.

Memory Stripping

Memory stripping involves describing every single facet of the focal point, no matter how small. After concentrating for a few seconds on your focal point, describe to your guide everything you can see or sense. Do not leave out any detail.

You may know more about the memory fragment than you volunteer. Rather than deliberately withholding information, you simply do not consider putting into words all of what you see or believe to be true. You leave out details because of the powerful no-talk rule that surrounds abuse or because you are dealing with abuse that happened to you when you were pre-verbal, when awareness far outstrips words.

Because of this tendency to leave out details, your guide should follow up your description of your focal point with questions to fill in any blanks. The guide envisions whatever you are describing and then plays a version of "what's missing from this picture?" The questions are designed only to get as complete a picture as possible, so remember that it is perfectly all right to say, "I don't know."

Kelly related as much as she could about her focal point. "I sense that this hand is pulling my much smaller hand toward her crotch. I don't really have a picture of this, only a feeling that it happened. I also get the sense of myself resisting the pull, like I don't want to let my arm move. I think I'm very young, maybe a year or year and a half old. That's all I can tell you about it."

Kelly was asked if it seemed like it was night or day and if she had any sense of where this was taking place? "It's night," she replied. "And we are in bed, under the covers." Did she have any sense of who the woman was or have any more information about her? "It's my mother," Kelly whispered, deep in her shame. "I hate to even say it, but it's my mother."

Sequencing

You must now move from image to action. What you are dealing with so far is only a portion of what happened. The focal point is, in effect, a freeze-frame photograph of an event. You want to develop a sequenced slide show, showing the action from beginning to end.

The basic question your guide should ask is, "What happens next?" This question becomes a stimulus for the unconscious to begin producing related imagery that will tell you more about the abuse. Whenever you seem ready to move on to new imagery, some variant of the question, like "Then what happens?" or "And then . . . ?" will help you move on to new imagery.

When Kelly was asked what happened next, she was able to shift easily from describing a scene to sensing or picturing what the sequence of action was. "My mom tries to force my hand between her legs. I pull back, but not too hard, because I'm afraid of making her mad at me. I feel prickly hair against my hand, and then it feels slimy and wet and yucky."

By now Kelly was crying. "She uses my hand to rub herself. She pushes on my fingers to make me do it without her holding my hand, but I just keep my hand limp. Then she moans real loud, and I get the feeling she falls asleep."

Kelly was able to describe a sequence of events, but some of you will have a harder time letting yourself move from a still image to an action series. You may be hesitant because you are in a new situation and do not understand what is being asked of you. A few words of encouragement and a brief recap of the instructions from your guide should help you to move into this stage of imagistic work.

Some of you will misunderstand the process. Instead of letting yourself respond to the question of what happened next, you free associate about the focal point. It reminds you of certain other memories from your past, and you begin jumping from one recall memory to another. This is essentially nonproductive. While free association has been known to facilitate spontaneous retrieval of repressed memories in psychoanalysis, the process is protracted and expensive.

You are not trying to stimulate your recall memories. Instead, you need to let yourself imagine or picture what might have happened to you. There is a difference between free association and letting yourself see whatever pops into your head. Let your right brain do the work.

(The left side of the brain is the side that performs analysis and deals in order and logic. It is best at handling time-related material that is linear. The right hemisphere is the creative, intuitive side of the brain that synthesizes experience. It is superior when what is experienced is difficult to describe in words. It is *this* part of yourself you want to access.)

Occasionally you may need a small verbal push to get started. Your guide may suggest some action that seems to arise naturally from the image you are picturing. For example, if a survivor has described seeing a dark silhouette standing in the doorway, watching her, her guide can prompt her by saying something like, "Let him come into the room." If no action suggestion seems obvious from the focal point, no prompting should be done.

All questions should be phrased in the present tense, just as they are with hypnosis and dream work. The unconscious operates only in the present; it does not deal in the past or the future. Your dreams, for example, are never set in the past or future within the dream itself. You may dream about something that happened to you in your past, but in the dream itself the incident occurs in the present. When doing guided imagistic work, you stay in the present because that is how the images present themselves to you.

Leading questions are also avoided. No matter how obvious the next step in the sequence may be, your guide should stick to neutral questions in the form of "What happens next?" This helps allay the inevitable belief that your guide is just putting the ideas in your head.

Your guide will seldom be able to imagine what you are about to say next. Therapists who do this work report over and over again that what they imagine is going to happen seldom does. They have a picture in their mind of what the next logical step in the action is, only to be completely taken aback by the sequence of events the survivor describes.

A horrifying example of memory turning in a surprising direction occurred with Vera, a survivor of sadistic and ritual abuse by her grandfather. Sadistic and ritual abuse is exceptionally brutal. While this example may be shocking to some, others have abusive backgrounds that are just as brutally violent.

Vera was remembering being tied spread-eagled on a table with her grandfather looming over her, holding a knife in one hand and a live rat in another. Knowing from years of experience that sadistic abusers of children often threaten them by mutilating an animal in front of them, her therapist nearly blurted out the question, "What does he do to the rat?"

Self-discipline prevailed, and instead the therapist said, "Tell me what happens next." Visibly shaking, Vera replied, "He cuts the rope from around my neck and starts to shove the rat in my mouth. I am squirming, trying to get away, and he says, 'Do you want the rat or me?' Then he puts his penis in my mouth. I hold real still because I don't want him to push the rat down my throat."

Sometimes in probing imagistic memory, the related images that you will experience are not sequential images. Instead, images of similar abusive episodes flood your mind, triggered by a stimulus in the imagery that is common to other times you were abused. Usually the images are clearly contradictory, such as portrayals of two different ages, or two different locales.

Sandra was describing a persistent image she had of her parents driving away, leaving her at her grandparents' farm. She recounted going in the house where her grandfather was lying on the couch. Then she said, "I see him pulling me on his lap. I can even see what I have on. It's a blue-checked sunsuit. But that couldn't be true, because they didn't move to the farm until I was six. I had that sunsuit before I went to kindergarten."

When the imagery is confusing, you may be mixing images from more than one abusive incident. If you sense that you are doing that, choose only one of the images for now, reminding yourself that you can always work on the contradictory image in another session. Select the image that is the clearest or most compelling and make that your focal point.

Sandra chose to focus on the imagery of her grandparents' farm, since watching her parents drive away was so hauntingly clear to her. She worked through her grandfather's sexual molestation on the couch at the farmhouse, and in her next session she returned to the image of sitting on his lap wearing the blue sunsuit. Another memory of being abused by him surfaced. Although the second memory occurred at a different age and in a different house, both memories involved being molested while being held on her grandfather's lap.

Resistance

Once through the initial pitfalls, sequencing pro-
ceeds smoothly for a time. You will be able to freely
share your images and awarenesses. Action builds, and
you become deeply engaged in the process, curious to
find out what your mind will picture.

Resistance to the memories eventually sets in, for
closely guarded psychic secrets are not easily breached.
Resistance takes the form of thoughts or actions that
obstruct the process of retrieving memories. When you
resist, you are consciously convinced that the reason for
stopping or questioning the process is valid. Your unconscious motive, however, is protection of yourself
and your family.

Resistance takes many forms, but it most often occurs at certain specific points in imagistic work. Three
critical junctures in the emergence of memories seem to
be especially vulnerable to resistance: before the initial
act of sexual abuse, before the most traumatic act of
sexual abuse, and after the most traumatic act. Resistance surges at these times.

Before the initial act of sexual abuse, you are most
likely to stop the process by saying something like,
"That's all I can remember." You have set the scene,
and a sequence of events has begun. Perhaps the dark
figure in the doorway is now in the room, leaning over
the bed, and the covers have been pulled off the
frightened child. Suddenly you shut down. "That's as
far as I can go," you claim. "I can't see anymore."

This is never the case. Invariably patience pays off,
and you will be able to go beyond your self-imposed
block. Your guide may help by suggesting something
like, "Let yourself know what you need to know about
this." You will usually be able to take the step of moving ahead with the work.

Before the most traumatic act of sexual abuse, you are susceptible to creating a premature ending to the abuse, with what is known as a "rescue fantasy." Young children use rescue fantasies quite blatantly. Four- or five-year-olds are earnestly telling about their abuse, when it suddenly gets too frightening. To handle the fear, they make up a rescue, usually by some super-hero who comes and locks up the bad guy.

Adults are more sophisticated in their rescue fantasies. You may picture your mother coming in the room, the offender losing interest and leaving, or yourself successfully telling the offender to stop. Your guide may be able to hear a slight note of relief in your voice, and the abuse ends without the perpetrator completing an act of sexual abuse.

People do not generally repress memories of aborted attempts at sexual abuse. Whenever something like this happens in imagistic work, your guide may need to remind you of the existence of rescue fantasies. He or she may then suggest that you let the offender come back into the scene, and then continue to do sequencing work. Usually, you will be able to move past your idealized view of the abuse situation into a scene you sense is more authentic.

The most traumatic act of the abuse is usually the act that culminates in the orgasm of the offender. At this point, you are completely dissociated from the scenes you are picturing, even if you had strong feelings and body memories earlier. The dissociation makes what you are describing seem completely unreal, and you may say such things as, "I must be making this up," or "I'm just saying what you want me to say."

Repressed memories rarely seem real when they first emerge. You will not be able to judge whether it is real. You may have to test the reality of your abuse memories for a year or more before you can come to any conclusion about their validity.

Closure

After the offender finishes whatever sexual act he or she is committing, you will want to withdraw from the memory work. This withdrawal is counterproductive to the healing process. The unconscious always operates in the present tense, and, when a memory is buried in the unconscious, the unconscious preserves it as an ongoing act of abuse in the present reality of the unconscious mind. The cost of repressing a memory is that the mind does not know the abuse ended.

Uncompleted memory fragments continue to haunt you. Thus, you need to be encouraged to continue with sequencing until you and the offender are separated or normal activity is resumed. If you persevere until the abuse memory reaches closure, you will generally feel less chaotic and frightened than if you simply stop at the end of the sexual assault or let the scene fade out.

The session ends with a discussion about how you feel about the memory work. You may also want to strategize about handling surges of denial or waves of feelings about the memory. If you have a tendency toward self-destructive behavior, be sure to devise a protection plan with your therapist for as long as needed.

THE AFTERMATH

It is vitally important to monitor what happens in the few days or weeks after memory work. The feelings that come after retrieving a memory are memories, too. Your feeling state and your behavior directly relate to how you felt and behaved after the original abuse.

Lynn, for example, was a survivor who had been abused by her adolescent brother until he left home when she was six. Lynn was a gregarious woman, and she always mobilized her extensive support network each time she recovered another memory. She would tell her friends and Twelve-Step group what she remembered in detail, eliciting positive feedback and much needed protective responses.

One session, however, she worked on a memory in which her older sister, who was a young adult at the time of the abuse, came upon Lynn being pinched, pummeled, and orally assaulted by her brother behind the house. Her sister told her brother that she was going to tell their mother, grabbed Lynn, and marched off, tight-lipped and silent. Not another word was spoken about the scene she had encountered.

In the few weeks after retrieving this memory, Lynn got very depressed. She did not tell any of her friends about her memory work and isolated herself from them socially. She was withdrawn and quiet even in her therapy sessions. It was not until she realized that she was acting out just what happened after her sister found her that she was able to return to her usual gregarious nature. Her silence was a memory, too.

EMPOWERING YOURSELF

Prepare a list of possible focal points you would use if you decided to do imagistic work. Include blips, dream images, objects you are afraid of, and anything else that seems suitable. Review your list from Chapter Five for possible focal points.

Imagistic work requires collaboration with another person who has some skill in doing memory work. You may want to talk over doing imagistic work with your therapist, or with someone else who might be appropriate. If you do not have someone who could help you with this, you may want to read the section on journal writing in Chapter Eight and apply these techniques to your writing.

CHAPTER SEVEN

DREAM WORK

Sarah often had nightmares, which she recorded in her dream journal to work with as part of her therapy. One in particular disturbed her deeply. Since having this dream, she had been feeling acutely anxious, and she was becoming increasingly afraid to go outdoors. She sensed the dream contained important information about her abuse.

"In the dream I'm walking down a deserted neighborhood street on a bright, sunny day. Suddenly I hear the noise of a motor a couple of blocks away. A large, slow-moving machine comes into view. It is sort of a wooden platform on wheels, with a huge metal engine sitting on it. There is a funnel-like opening into the engine, and a man is standing on the platform, sticking tree branches into the funnel as he guides the machine down the street.

"The man spots me. Then his eyes shift, as he quickly scans the neighborhood to see if anyone is around. He's instantly aware of my vulnerability, that there is no one to help me. He is completely cold and calculating. I can sense his satisfaction that I am at his mercy. It's clear that he is going to murder me.

"I get absolutely terrified when I see him assessing the situation. I look around for the nearest house I can run to. I stare at the closest one, but it is futile. I will never make it before he catches me, and both of us realize that. The dream ends with me knowing I'm as good as dead."

The first thing that caught my attention was a recurring theme. Sarah's nightmare happened on a bright, sunny day. Her first panic attack occurred on a bright, sunny day, and, in her imagistic work, Sarah had said that she was surprised at how sunny and pretty the world was when she came out of the outhouse after the abuse by her grandfather. It appeared as though her grandfather had especially enjoyed abusing her on lovely, sunny days. Like so many psychopaths, he enjoyed hurting her when the world was brightest and she was carefree.

I next asked her to elaborate on her description of the odd machine in her dream. "The platform and wheels and the way the man is standing on the machine remind me of those railroad hand cars you used to see. But the engine part is more like a woodchopper, the kind they use to chop up tree branches into little bits. The floor of the machine is covered with small pieces of wood spit out by the engine."

When I asked her where she used to see railroad cars, Sarah told me her grandfather lived next to railroad tracks. Sensing the link between the locale of the dream and her grandfather's home, she volunteered that there was a woodpile next to the outhouse where her grandfather used to chop up the wood into smaller pieces. "There was a pile of wood chips from the chopping that looked just like the pile on the machine!"

The woodchopper man was a dream symbol for Sarah's grandfather. The theme of the dream was somehow his abuse of Sarah. We could perhaps learn more about Sarah's history, or at least get some important clues, if we looked more closely at some of the details in the nightmare.

I asked her if her dream vision "zoomed in" and showed a close-up of one part of the dream. She replied, "The man standing on the woodchopper has deep brown eyes. When he glances around to assess his chances of getting me without anyone seeing him, I can see how his eyes shift without his head moving. That was the most chilling and most detailed part of the dream."

With a flash of insight, she said, "My grandfather had brown eyes like that — flat and dead-looking." She started crying. "I think he used to catch me outdoors. When he wanted to abuse me, he would give that quick, assessing glance around to see if he could get away with it. That look always told me something horrible was going to happen. I felt like a trapped, hunted animal."

Sarah had discovered what she needed to know from her dream. Not only were her symptoms, imagery, and feelings all telling her that her grandfather had abused her but her dream world was signaling her too. Her unconscious was validating her repressed memories.

She now had the wisdom of her dream to help her understand more about the nature of the abuse she suffered. She could make a link between her fear of going outdoors and her grandfather's silent stalking of her. He had easy access to her when she was sent outdoors to play. Sunny days and the outdoors held real terror for the little girl inside Sarah.

The swift glance around that her grandfather made was Sarah's signal that the abuse would start. Knowing this was vital to her recovery, for it is in the small but significant details that our suffering becomes evident to us. Sarah was able to get in touch with her paralyzing fear and helplessness through this part of the dream. It was also so specific that it added further validation to the reality of her memories.

USING DREAMS IN YOUR RECOVERY

Dreams are both a physiological and a psychological process. Dreams occur regularly, approximately every ninety minutes during sleep, and they are a measurable physical reaction during sleep that is necessary to our well-being. We do not remember most of these dreams. They are part of an involuntary, sometimes random, psychic process.

The dreams we do remember, however, usually embody a symbolic message from our unconscious about our emotional life. As Carl Jung said in his *Collected Works,* "The dream gives a true picture of the subjective state, while the conscious mind denies that this state exists or recognizes it only grudgingly." Paying attention to the messages in dreams can enlighten us about areas of our lives that are too complex or difficult to face consciously.

Beware of pat statements about what a dream means. Many people make the mistake of believing that there is some universal list of what the symbols in dreams represent. "Dreams of flying are dreams about sex," these self-styled dream masters tell you authoritatively. "And dreams about fire are always about anger."

This is a trap in dream work. There is no precise, approved list of what the symbols in dreams mean, for the symbolism is unique to the individual dreamer. True, there are some symbols that hold common meaning for many people—snakes really do represent penises for a lot of people. Still, for some snakes might mean evil, or solitude, or sneakiness. No matter how com-

mon the symbol, each dream must always be understood within the context of the individual dreamer.

Some dreams are symbolic in nature, referring to
deep emotional issues in symbolic form. Other dreams,
however, are repressed memory dreams. These dreams
contain vital information about repressed memories. If
worked with appropriately, they provide a direct link
to the buried memories.

Symbolic Dreams

Symbolic dreams are encoded messages from the
unconscious about your past or present emotional life.
Through symbols, they make oblique references to the
feelings that you have hidden from yourself. They
broaden your perspective on problems and help you
reach new levels of awareness. If you have the tools and
the openness to decode your symbolic dreams, they are
a rich source of wisdom.

Judy had a wonderful symbolic dream while em-
broiled in a pitched power struggle with her husband
over some seemingly vital domestic matter. That night
she fell asleep going over and over her position, convinced that resolving the issue was somehow vital to
her well-being. Her unconscious offered her a dream in
which she and her husband were heatedly playing a
board game. When she woke up, she realized the game
they were playing in her dream was Trivial Pursuit.
Judy shared her dream with her husband, and, laughing,
they resolved the issue in a matter of minutes.

Symbolic dreams are dreams about your emotional
life. You need to work with them to find out what the
symbolism in the dream means about your growth, or
what it tells you about blocks to your growth. Symbolic
dreams can help you get in touch with your inner child
or with deep conflicts you have about your life, your
parents, your sexuality, your career. They highlight

feelings you may wish to avoid, like rage, shame, lone-liness, or sadness.

Kylie was a lovely young woman who felt she was "stuck." She seemed unable to get past a certain point in recovering her memories. After three days of hard work on memory retrieval, Kylie came in with a dream.

"In the dream I was driving my car straight up a cliff. It was absolutely perpendicular, straight up and down. When I got near the top, I couldn't get the wheels over the edge onto level ground. The motor was grinding and grinding, but the car just couldn't make that last few feet. Then I saw that even if I could get the car up and over, there was an older woman sitting in her car a few feet back from the top of the cliff, com-pletely blocking my way. She was just looking at me, staring. I realized I would never get up there, so I turned the car sideways and drove to another place where I could go up."

Kylie's dream symbolized her mother's blockage of her growth in therapy. While her mother had never really spoken out against Kylie's therapy or her re-pressed memories of abuse, the dream revealed the power her nonverbal messages had in stopping Kylie. The grim stare of the woman in the dream reminded Kylie of her mother's implacable stare whenever Kylie brought up her therapy. In her dream Kylie found a way around the older woman's car, and in her therapy she found a way around her mother's power to block her memories and her growth.

With symbolic dreams ask, "What does this dream have to say about my life or feelings?" Pay attention to the theme of the dream, the setting, and the characters in the dream. Is the dream about a journey, a feeling, a child, a family, a sense of being lost? Whatever the dream seems to be about, try to picture it as a metaphor for your life, and allow yourself to experience your feel-ings about the dream.

Repressed Memory Dreams

Repressed memory dreams are dreams that contain a partial repressed memory or symbols that provide access to a repressed memory. During sleep, you have a direct link to your unconscious. Because the channel is open, memory fragments or symbols from repressed sexual abuse memories often intrude into the dream state. Even though the memory is embedded in the symbolism of the dream world, it is possible to use the dream to retrieve the memory.

Sarah's nightmare is a good example of a repressed memory dream that alludes to repressed memories. The presence of a murderous psychopath, the paralyzing sense of fear, and the acute post-dream anxiety are all signals that her dream is about a traumatic event. When Sarah worked on the dream, her own associations to her grandfather's abuse led inevitably to her abuse memories as core to the meaning of the dream.

Repressed memory dreams are an invaluable tool in the recovery of memories. You first need to know which types of dreams are likely to contain memory fragments encapsulated in the dream. Once you identify a dream as a repressed memory dream, you can then ask, "What does this dream tell me about how I was abused?"

TYPES OF DREAMS CONTAINING REPRESSED MEMORIES

There are several kinds of dreams you need to assess carefully in regard to repressed memories. These are the dreams most likely to give you significant information about your abuse history. Remember, though, that you know the most about your dream world. If you have a dream that does not seem to fit this list but you believe contains a memory fragment, trust yourself.

Nightmares

Nightmares are dreams that frighten you by presenting you with symbols of your deepest fears. Usually you feel frightened while in the dream state, but sometimes you are fearful only when you contemplate the dream after you awake. A recent poll found that the average American has one nightmare a year. If you have PTSD, in all likelihood, you have far more nightmares than that.

Nightmares are common purveyors of repressed memories. The distinguishing feature is the intensity of the fear you experience around the dream, and repressed memories of sexual abuse hold much terror. Other types of dreams may also be nightmares, in addition to being classed as recurring dreams, childhood dreams, and so on.

Certain elements in nightmares are indicators that a nightmare may be about sexual abuse. The types of people who are likely to commit sexual abuse, such as rapists, murderers, psychopaths, or stalkers, are commonly found in nightmares about repressed memories. The places where sexual abuse frequently occurs—bedrooms, bathrooms, basements, closets, or attics—are often the settings for nightmares referencing sexual abuse. Things used to sexually abuse are important indicators, such as penises, breasts, buttocks, bottles, broom handles, and sticks.

Ritual abuse survivors often have nightmares with ritual symbols or satanic overtones. Dreams of blood, sacrifice, torture, dismemberment, or other grisly themes may indicate repressed memories of ritual abuse. Nightmares about Satan, the devil, chanting, menacing robed figures, cannibalism, or other satanic symbols should be carefully assessed in terms of ritual cult abuse.

Recurring Dreams

These are dreams that you have over and over again, with virtually no change in the characters, action, or setting. They are often nightmares, but even nonthreatening recurring dreams are an emergency signal from your unconscious. The signal keeps repeating until you respond to the message by dealing with the issue imbedded in the dream. Recurring dreams often indicate an unresolved sexual abuse trauma.

Dreams You Remember from Your Childhood

You may have had a childhood dream only once, or it may have been a recurring dream. In any case, it made such a strong impression on you that you never forgot it. Your conscious mind agreed to aid your unconscious by keeping the dream memory alive until you had the strength to face its true meaning. Often a dream you remember vividly from your childhood is a major clue to buried memories of abuse.

Sexual Abuse Dreams

Dreams containing an explicit act or theme of sexual abuse need to be carefully scrutinized. In my clinical experience, these are always repressed memory dreams. The setting, the action, or the dream characters may have symbolic aspects, but the dream contains a specific, clear-cut act of sexual abuse. A memory fragment from the repressed sexual abuse shows up undiluted in the dream state, surrounded by the symbolism of the dream world.

Sexual dreams are not the same thing as sexual abuse dreams. Sexual dreams are characterized by pleasurable sexual contact that is age-appropriate and without any theme of force, illegality, or pain. Sexual abuse dreams may or may not be experienced as pleasurable by the dreamer. Some are nightmares, while others involve highly charged erotic feelings. Sexual abuse dreams contain acts of, or threats of, sexual victimization, such as rape, oral or anal sexual violation, molestation of a child or teen, voyeurism, or bestiality.

Barbara was an intelligent, competent woman who had been in therapy for several years working on memories of her father's molestation of her. She had an investment in believing that his abuse stopped short of intercourse. She asserted, "I'm just not that damaged."

A dream challenged Barbara's protective assumption. She dreamt that an older man was taking a young woman or girl on a tour of a castle, which would be their home after they married. When the man showed her the master bedroom, he began to make love to the girl/woman on the floor. At first she was willing, but when the man attempted intercourse, the girl resisted. The harder she struggled, the more aggressive the man became.

Then the girl/woman began to shrink, until she was only three feet high. The man raped her, and the focus of the dream was on his forcing his penis into her very small vagina. The physical pain was intense, and she began moaning and moving her head in pain. She was aware that the man was frustrated with trying to achieve an orgasm while refraining from penetrating her fully and ripping her badly. The dream ended with her experience of pain when the man thrust too far.

Barbara's dream began in a symbolic setting with symbolic characters, but it contained an act of rape and an intense, painful body memory of that rape. "How could I know so well what it was like to be penetrated by someone who was trying to reach orgasm but had to use only the very tip of the penis?" Barbara cried. "How could I know how much that hurt a very small vagina, especially when he would get overexcited and lose control? That must have happened to me!" Over several grueling sessions, she came to believe that her father had raped her when she was very small.

Dreams Containing Access Symbols

These are dreams with a set of symbols that point to the existence of a buried memory. The dream world acknowledges the abuse obliquely instead of directly, through symbolic representations of the forgotten abuse. Working with the symbols provides access to the associated repressed memory.

In addition to the symbols already mentioned in the section on nightmares, secrets, closed or locked doors, mysterious passageways, or anything stored or hidden are frequent access symbols. The appearance of a child in a dream, particularly one who cannot communicate or whom you are trying to protect, is another common access symbol. Water, especially water that frightens you, can be an access symbol in dreams, often symbolizing sexual abuse in a bathing situation. Snakes or other phallic symbols are often references to abuse involving someone's penis.

John had been apathetic and mildly depressed for most of his adult life. His childhood was a blank to him, until one night he dreamed about an attic. "I was in a huge attic, running away from someone who was trying to hurt me. I had to climb over huge, boulder-size crates that were locked and strapped tight. I knew they contained information that I was not supposed to have, and I didn't want to be caught near them. The farther I ran, the longer the attic seemed to get. I was terrified I would never get out of there."

In his dream work, John focused on one of the crates and pictured himself unlocking it. When he did so, he got a clear picture of himself being physically and sexually abused by his older brother. Although this was a painful revelation, almost immediately he began to show more interest in not only his therapy but also his life. John's energy had been so drained by repressing the "crates" of information about his abuse that he had little energy to use in the present.

Sometimes the access symbol your unconscious selects as a focus is idiosyncratic to your abuse history. The symbol itself does not alert you, but the intensity of the dream or the repetition of the symbol in several dreams is a red flag. Mona, for example, was a survivor who often dreamed about chickens. Her "chicken dreams" were not nightmares, but she felt strongly that their meaning was important. When she finally did imagistic work using the chickens in one dream as a focal point, Mona discovered she had been abused by an uncle during a family gathering to butcher chickens. Once she retrieved this memory, her "chicken dreams" stopped.

Any Dream You Have a Strong Feeling About

Sometimes we have dreams that may seem uninteresting or trivial to others, but they are especially vivid to us. The dreams seems to be highlighted for us by our unconscious. One survivor described it well by saying, "Even though my dream appeared ordinary, there seemed to be silent background music playing. It was like in the movies when the hero is simply walking down the hall, but scary music is playing, telling you to pay attention." Any dream that seems to have made a strong impression on you may well have elements of repressed memory in it.

RETRIEVING REPRESSED MEMORIES FROM DREAMS

Analyzing a dream always seems to be a formidable task at first glance, especially if you suspect it has a repressed memory attached to it. You become convinced that the dream has a concrete, verifiable meaning, and, whatever the meaning, it will surely elude you. In actuality, the dream's message or memory will always be repeated in your dreams until you grasp what you need to know.

Always approach dreams with an awareness that it is perfectly acceptable to never find the "true" meaning of any particular dream. Simply to listen and appreciate the dream world of the dreamer is healing in itself. Once free from trying to understand the dream, you can begin to explore the dream without fear.

Exploring your dreams is a journey best made with a partner. You are trying to unmask your unconscious, your hidden side. A trustworthy guide, whether a sensitive friend or skilled therapist, will not have the blind spots and reluctance you do in facing your unconscious. If you and your therapist have not done dream work before, openly discuss your interest in doing this kind of work. If he or she is not interested or skilled in this area, ask for a referral to someone who does work with dreams or discuss doing this work with a sensitive friend as your guide.

Talk over your expectations and any fears you might have with your guide. Try to get a sense of how he or she views dreams in relationship to repressed memories. You may want to suggest reading this chapter as a starting point in clarifying how you will work together on your dreams.

There are many structured and unstructured ways of using dreams to uncover or clarify repressed memories. The following description of a general dream work process will help you get an idea of how you might proceed, but be open to different methods and creative approaches. Adjust your approach to that of your guide, remembering that there are countless ways to approach the unconscious reality revealed through the dream world.

Listen

In using dreams to retrieve repressed memories, you need to deliberately assess the symbolism and dream story in light of possible sexual abuse. Look very actively for clues about your abuse history in the dream. Once you have processed the dream in this way, you can choose from a variety of dream work methods to further probe the dream for repressed memories.

Listening to the dream with all your senses on alert is the first and most important step in retrieving repressed memories. As you tell your dream or read a description of it from your dream journal, you and your guide listen for themes or symbols of sexual abuse, for oddities, for unusual figures of speech, for anything that catches your attention or causes curiosity. Anything that seems to refer to abuse or anything you do not understand can possibly be a repressed memory fragment.

Next share your interpretation of the dream. The feelings and thoughts you have are vital to understanding your experience of the dream. Once you have shared what you think the dream means, listen as your guide shares what he or she heard when you told your dream.

Clarify

The next stop is to illuminate the dream. Your guide should ask you clarifying questions so that both of you arrive at a deeper understanding of the dream's symbolism. Whatever your guide cannot picture clearly from your description or whatever seems to even hint at possible sexual abuse becomes the focus for questioning.

Clarifying questions are asked for information, expansion, or association. Information questions clear up any confusions your guide has about the plot, development, or sequence of the dream. For example, he or she might ask, "Did the man come into your bedroom while you were asleep or when you were awake?" Expansion questions allow you to expand on a particular symbol or action in the dream. Your guide might say, "Tell me more about the house you were trapped in. Describe it for me." Association questions ask, "What, does this part of the dream remind you of? What does it make you think of?"

When people from the dreamer's life appear, your guide should always ask something like, "What is the first thing you think of when you picture this person? What role does this person have in your life?" No matter how obscure the person, he or she is in the dream for a reason. Asking you to free-associate about the person helps you to understand the person's appearance in the dream.

The vividness of the dream is important. Are any parts of the dream more prominent or more vivid? Do the intensity of the feelings in the dream increase at any point? Often the vividness of a dream will highlight the portion that contains a memory fragment.

Your guide should also ask about the zoom feature of the dream camera. The zoom feature is a close-up shot of some detail in the dream. As in the movies, the close-up in dreams is always inserted for a purpose. In repressed memory dreams, what is zoomed in on is often some detail from the abuse that you focused on while being abused.

Carl had a dream that made no sense to him until he was asked about the zoom feature. In his dream was a bewildering array of people meandering in and out of a kitchen area. Carl was being asked to do something he did not understand, and he had the sense that not to comply would mean certain death to a group of people outside the kitchen area. The dream ended on a fade-out with no resolution.

When he was asked about any close-ups, he said, "At one point the leader of this group asked me to step up and talk to him. I was really frightened. There was a zoom-in on the step I had to stand on to talk to him. It was a gray wooden step. I can see it clearly even now."

When asked what the first thing that popped into his mind was when he thought about the step, Carl said, "The step in my uncle's kitchen. His kitchen had a stair-case to the upstairs, and the first step up was a three-foot square landing." As he talked, Carl began to get images of himself being cornered and orally abused by his uncle on that step.

Identify

After you and your guide have ransacked the dream for knowledge, you need to identify what the dream tells you about your repressed memories. Pool your perceptions to identify any memory fragments that seem to have intruded directly into the dream. You also need to pinpoint any access symbols, which may provide entry to buried memories.

Usually the process of listening to and clarifying the dream results in at least one memory fragment coming to the foreground. Any act of sexual abuse is high-lighted, of course, as are any of the symbols mentioned in the sections on nightmares and theme dreams. Any other part of the dream that either of you think might contain a memory fragment or that might provide access to one is acknowledged, too.

Diane knew she had been severely abused by her father. She came to her group one day with a dream that she felt certain referred to her abuse because of its intensity. In the dream, she was on her hands and knees in a kitchen, washing the floor. Floating in the air were green U-shaped neon objects. Her father was standing next to a large mirror over the sink, watching her. The dream had no action but was marked by a sense of desperate fear.

As she clarified the dream, Diane made a number of associations to the kitchen in the house where she was a teenager. She remembered how she had to scrub the floor on her hands and knees every evening. The kitchen also had a large mirror over the sink. She expanded on her description of the green neon objects, explaining that they were elongated tubes of neon and there were three or four of them.

When the group listened to Diane's dream, they identified the mirror over the sink, her father staring at her, and her pose in the dream as possible memory fragments. Group members were particularly struck by the oddity of the green neon objects, speculating that this might be an access symbol. Everyone agreed with Diane's sense that this was a repressed memory dream.

When asked to identify what the dream told her about her abuse, Diane's answer was very specific. "I think my father raped me in the evenings when I was cleaning the kitchen and my mother was getting drunk in the living room. He would make me crawl around naked while he watched in the mirror. I also believe the green neon things are about a time he put a cucumber in me." Later imagistic work added more details to this repressed memory, but Diane had identified the general outline from her dream work.

Directed Memory Work

Dream work with a repressed memory dream sometimes precipitates spontaneous memory recovery. You may be flooded with memories of the abusive incident embedded in the dream as it is clarified. Imagistic, feeling, or body memories are the forms of memory most often triggered by dream work. Recall or acting-out memories are triggered less often.

Many times, however, you will benefit from further work on the dream in a structured way that elicits the repressed memory directly. The dream symbols provide clues or information on the abuse, but a cohesive picture of what precisely happened is almost never spelled out in the dream. To achieve this, you need to do directed memory work.

You need to keep an ongoing written list of any memory fragments or access symbols that emerge from your dream world. When you are ready to do memory work, review the list of memory fragments and access symbols and select a part of the dream to work on. Usually one section of the dream emerges as central, or a certain symbol seems especially prominent. Once you know what part of the dream you want to explore for repressed memories, select a method of memory retrieval.

Imagistic work or journal writing are often the most effective methods of direct memory work with dreams. These two methods seem to retrieve repressed memories more quickly and more completely for the greatest number of survivors. If your preference is to do hypnosis, art therapy, body work, or feelings work with a dream segment, proceed with one of those processes. Whatever you choose, use the symbolism of the dream as the focal point of the process.

EMPOWERING YOURSELF

If you do not already keep a dream journal, you may want to start one now. Keep it near your bed, and write down your dreams as soon as you wake up. Start with recording any dreams you remember from your child-

hood, and then move on to any particularly vivid
dreams you have had recently. Once these have been
recorded, you are ready to keep a record of your present
dreams.

You can also prime your dream pump, so to speak.
Before you go to sleep at night, visualize yourself as a
little child. Tell your inner child that she or he is safe
now and that it is all right to tell you about what happened. Then suggest that your inner child show you in
a dream what you need to know about the abuse. Try
this exercise for at least a week and discipline yourself
to write down the dreams you remember during that
week. You may want to do this for an even longer
period of time.

Select a dream that you think is a repressed memory.
After you have written down the dream, go through it,
marking or underlining any symbol or segment of the
dream that seems to contain information about your
repressed memories. With your therapist or a trusted
friend, go over the dream, using your own process or
the steps outlined earlier. Then write in your journal or
verbalize what you learned from the dream about how
you were abused.

CHAPTER EIGHT

ALTERNATIVE
STRATEGIES

Sarah began seeing a massage therapist experienced in working with repressed memories. During one of her sessions with this talented woman, she had a body memory. While the therapist was working on her feet, Sarah felt intense discomfort, especially around her toenails. She cried during this part of the massage and refused to let her feet be touched in subsequent massages.

After the massage experience, she had a dream that bothered her. The dream had a zoom feature of a bowl of water with wood chips floating in it. Sarah used this dream image as a focal point and quickly wrote in her journal whatever came to her mind, without stopping to analyze.

In our next session, Sarah read what she had written. "Focus on the bowl of water with wood chips. He put my feet in the bowl. The water was cold. Then he took the wood chips and washed me, pushing some of them between my labia. White enamel metal bowl. Washing off my feet. Pushed a chip between my toenail and toe. I cried. Very real body sense of how cold the water was. My underpants got wet. He took them off and hid them."

Although some of what Sarah had written was confusing, it could not be dismissed. The zoom feature in dreams often highlights what survivors focused on during their abuse as an autohypnotic technique to distract themselves from pain. Sarah's dream showed a close-up of the bowl of water, and she focused back on the bowl of water in her journal writing when the wood chips were being pushed into her labia and under her toenail. The dream and her journal writing revealed her use of this dissociative process.

Sarah interpreted what she had written. "After I wrote this, I felt like I knew exactly what happened in this memory. Maybe I'm wrong, but the feelings and images were so strong and clear. I swear I could sense the temperature of the water so clearly that I could duplicate that exact temperature.

"I think my grandfather was supposed to wash my feet off before I could go in the house. They were dirty from going barefoot. He filled the bowl with water from the well and added a handful of small wood chips. My sense is he did this because he didn't have a washcloth, and the chips would help get the dirt off.

"He started washing my feet, sort of splashing the water and rubbing the dirt off with the chips. Then he started getting excited and washed higher and higher. He pulled aside the crotch of my underpants and started pushing the chips around my genital area.

"My underpants got wet and he took them off and hid them behind the bushes. I know this sounds crazy, but when I was doing this writing, I got a strong sense that he was hiding them so he could fondle them or masturbate with them later. I also get a strong image that they were training pants, so I think I was maybe two or two-and-a-half.

"I sense he liked hurting me. He took a small wood chip and forced it under my toenail. When I cried, my

*grandma came out, and he shook me by the arm, like I
was crying over having to be cleaned up."*

Sarah had discovered that journal writing and body
work were useful tools in the recovery of her repressed
memories. The memory she retrieved had more clarity
and validity than her previous work. While this was due
in part to Sarah's increasing capacity to search out and
piece together her memories, journal writing and body
work are two very powerful techniques. Along with
hypnosis, feelings work, and art therapy, they offer a
variety of viable therapeutic choices to survivors working on their memories.

Each strategy works better for some survivors than
others, depending on personal style and the way you
process the world. A highly tactile person will do very
well with body work, while someone who has a violent
trauma response to touch will do best to avoid it. A
visually creative person will thrive on art therapy, while
a person who loves the release that writing gives will
seek out journal writing. Select what suits you best,
turning to other methods if you need change. There is
never only one path up the mountain.

All five of these approaches are forms of therapy
with much broader application than memory recovery
work. Each one can be used as the sole form of therapy
for many problems. While this chapter will only review
how these strategies can be useful to retrieve repressed
memories, you may want to use them to help you heal
in a wide variety of ways.

Journal writing is available to anyone, any time of
the day or night, but the other strategies generally require a trained professional with specific skills. You
may be limited by who is available in your community.
You will also need to exercise caution in selecting a

professional to work with. Many professionals with expertise in one of these areas may not have acquired techniques that apply specifically to uncovering repressed abuse memories.

Other experts will have developed creative applications to uncovering memories that go far beyond what is suggested in this chapter. Techniques for memory recovery are as unlimited as human creativity. This chapter is intended only as an overview, not as a definitive list of how these strategies should be used. Stay open to new approaches, provided they work for you and your boundaries are respected.

JOURNAL WRITING

Journal writing is the most effective way to recover memories for some survivors, and it has a valuable place in the memory process for most others. Your journal operates as a twenty-four-hour therapist. It is always "on call" when a memory fragment emerges or your energy guides you toward working on a dream or image. You can turn to your journal as an avenue to your unconscious any hour of the day or night.

As a technique, journal writing is similar to imagistic work, substituting writing for words. Although there are different approaches to retrieving memories with journal writing, all of them start with a focal point to begin accessing the unconscious. You then write whatever emerges from your unconscious about the focal point. The blank pages act as your prompter, eliminating the need for a guide.

Journal writing utilizes acting-out memory. A focal point can be an access symbol from a dream, an image from a memory fragment, a body sensation, or simply the felt sense that an abusive memory is trying to surface. Starting from that point, you permit yourself to "act out" what you know about your abuse through writing.

Other kinds of memory are activated as you use acting-out memory to access your unconscious. You start out by using acting-out memory, but you may also get images, body memories, and feeling memories as well. When that happens, you use the writing as a way to record whatever images or messages you are receiving from your unconscious.

The writing must be done quickly, without censorship. You need to keep the pen moving, even if you have to push yourself to do so. Logic, spelling, and grammar must be ignored. To rely on acting-out memory, you must bypass that part of you that is a literary critic. Some survivors prefer to use their left hand to facilitate accessing of the right brain, but this is a matter of personal preference, not a necessity.

There are three basic techniques that are helpful in retrieving repressed memories using journal writing. You can adapt them for your own use or create your own strategies. Journal writing is a very flexible tool.

Free Association

Free association writing begins with a focal point and involves writing down whatever comes to you about that focal point. You must stay open to the images, feelings, body sensations, and words that float into your awareness and quickly jot them down. It helps to think of your writing arm simply as a recording instrument to help you avoid trying to impose order on what you are experiencing. Remember to write down whatever you sense, as well as what you are thinking.

Sarah used free association writing to retrieve her memory of the abuse with the wood chips. She wrote down exactly what she was experiencing as she experienced it, instead of trying to sort it out as it came to her. Her sorting-out process occurred after she had done the writing. Sorting out is a right brain process. If you do it while tapping into the unconscious, you impede the left brain from accessing what you want to know.

Storytelling

With this approach, you begin with a focal point and try to "write a story" about it. You can begin by writing something general like, "Once when I was little . . ." or "A little girl got abused by . . ." The object is to quickly write a scenario about an abusive incident.

The unconscious can be relied on to select traumatic incidents from your own past for most or all of the "story," since it is easier to rely on experience rather than imagination when you do something quickly. When you are finished, you can review what you wrote to see what fits for you. If you approach this writing with the goal of uncovering a repressed memory, most times you will find you have accessed your unconscious through acting-out memory in your writing.

Quick List

A quick list is a method that allows you to structure information about your abuse that is buried in your unconscious. With this technique, you quickly list your responses to a focal point or prompting question. Again, you must write your answers quickly, without thinking, screening, or editing.

Ann was a therapist herself, doing excellent work with survivors' repressed memories. When it came to her own memories, she was at sea. She knew her maternal grandmother had abused her from a few scattered recall memories and some very convincing dreams. The precise nature of the abuse—the when, where, and how —completely eluded her.

Trying imagistic work, hypnosis, and a referral to a massage therapy resulted in Ann being flooded with vague, amorphous imagery and sensations. She grew increasingly frustrated but refused to abandon her search, saying, "I feel like my life is on hold until I get this sorted out. I try to let it go, but I feel like a core part of me is missing. I want to know what it is."

Finally she tried a quick list. Her therapist handed her a pad and pencil and said, "I want you to quickly write down five things your grandmother did to you. Do it without pausing to think and don't worry about it being right. Quickly now, write down the first one."

After eight items she stopped. When she had finished, she had tears in her eyes. "Finally, I know," she said. Then she read her list.

"One. She pinched my genitals and stuck her finger in. Two. She made me suck on her breasts. Three. She hung my cat in front of me. Four. She held a pillow over my face and almost suffocated me. Five. She made me touch her between the legs. Six. She held my head under water when she bathed me. Seven. She pinched me all over, really hard. Eight. She stuck her finger in my rectum.

"I know there's more," Ann said after she finished. "But I feel like I at least have the basics of what happened. I'm sad, and kind of shocked, too, but at least now it's not so nebulous. I know I can go on from here."

BODY WORK

Body work involves the use of therapeutic massage or touch to aid in the release of feeling blockages centered in the body. When areas of your body that contain a body memory are subject to pressure, there is increased sensitivity in that area. Often imagistic, feeling, or acting-out memories are also stimulated. By sorting through the reactions your body has to the massage or touch, you can reconstruct a memory or a fragment of a memory.

Some major factors are important to consider in choosing a body work therapist. First, massage therapists vary in the intrusiveness of their style. Some take a very gentle, noninvasive approach to touch, while others work more aggressively with the body's resistance. While to a certain extent this is a matter of personal preference, no touching should ever involve great pain, nor should your genitals, nipples, or rectum ever be subject to any form of touch. Beware of rationalizations about physical pain or sexual touch offered by a perpetrator masquerading as a healer.

Body work specialists also vary a great deal in how well-equipped they are to handle the memories and feelings that are released during a healing massage. Some body work therapists are comfortable only with body work as a method to relieve muscle aches and stress and are not an appropriate choice for any therapy work. Others are listeners. They welcome emotional releases and verbal reports of what you are experiencing, but they offer little feedback or guidance about your internal process. Many professionals do, however, combine body work with empathic support to help you recover memories.

If you want to use body work to recover memories, be sure to carefully interview the people you are considering. Ask them about their training and approach to body work, so that you clearly know what parts of your body will be touched and in what manner. Discuss openly your interest in working with your repressed memories, and ascertain the professional's experience with this issue. If you do decide to work together, have a clear agreement about how the two of you will handle any feelings or body memories that come up.

Many survivors are deeply disturbed by the very thought of body work. Body work essentially involves impersonal touch, and impersonal touch is part of every act of sexual abuse. Survivors have learned, too, that any touch can ultimately turn into a sexual assault, no matter what role the touch is supposed to have in your life. Some find it very helpful to work through this issue with a caring professional, while others find the very idea of a stranger touching their body appalling. If you are not interested in or not ready for body work, that is a perfectly legitimate choice. Do not push yourself where you do not want to go.

Since there are numerous theories and approaches to body work, all of them cannot be detailed in this chapter. The following is a synthesis of how the process of recovering memories occurs with whatever physical approach is used. You may be able to decide from this overview if body work is an avenue you want to explore.

Energy

Memory recovery is based on the theory that the body stores memory as energy. Working with areas of the body where the energy is stored releases the energy. The therapist may simply lay his or her hands on your body, apply pressure, or massage your muscles. Whenever a part of your body is touched that was hurt, the stored or blocked energy can be accessed.

Emergence

The stored memory will emerge spontaneously if you are ready to face it. Emergence occurs in any number of ways. An area of your body may get hot or feel numb. You may hear something, or get a sudden image. Powerful emotions may sweep over you, causing you to weep or even cry out. The emergence may start out as only a vague sensation that something is different, or you can suddenly feel overwhelmed by sensation.

Sarah, for example, had an experience with body work when she was dealing with the physical abuse by her father. She was undergoing a passive form of body work involving laying on of hands when she had a slowly burgeoning sense of rage at her father for abusing her. This emotional experience was ready to emerge at this time in her life, and the touch released it.

Years later, massage therapy released another form of energy. The exquisite sensitivity Sarah had around her toes being touched was related to the memory of her grandfather shoving a wood chip under her toenail. When her feet were touched, she felt all the pain and the urge to scream and pull away that she had when the abuse first occurred. Her feet had been touched in her earlier work, but this memory was not ready to emerge.

Resolution

Maureen Morgan, a massage therapist, describes resolution as the ending of something that has to repeat itself in order to be resolved. The stored energy is released and what must be felt again is felt. What must be remembered again is remembered, and what must be surrendered is surrendered.

Ted was a survivor who used body work and therapy to recover memories. At one point in his massage therapy, he began to experience strange tingling sensations around his mouth and jaw. At first they happened only when his lower face was touched, but after a time, he would feel tingling and jolting sensations in his jaw even if his torso was touched.

When this would happen, he would sometimes get images of his father kicking him in the face, dislocating his jaw. Other pieces of memory emerged, all centered around his mouth and jaw. He talked in group therapy about oral sexual abuse by both parents. He had dreams about his mother jamming food down his throat when he was a very young child. He remembered his father using pliers to pull out teeth in a horrendously painful process.

All of these memories emerged through a nine-week period of body work focusing on his mouth, jaw, and face. As the body work continued, the memories flowed from Ted, consuming all his time in group therapy. As he raged about and grieved what had happened to him, the sensations during body work slowly faded. The tremendous stored energy was released and finally resolved.

HYPNOSIS

The general public thinks of hypnosis as the only way one recovers repressed memories. "I wish someone would just hypnotize me so I'd know what happened," is a common refrain I hear from survivors early in their therapy. They view hypnosis as magic, a mysterious power that acts like some sort of verbal "truth serum." Unfortunately, hypnosis is not magic. If it were, the issue of recovering memories would be a straightforward matter of therapeutic technique.

Hypnosis is effective only if you are ready to face what happened. What your unconscious produces during a trance state is that which is ready to emerge. You have fears and defenses that you need to work through before you are able to approach your memories through any technique.

If you are a very good hypnotic subject, and have a hypnotherapist who can help you with your own defenses, you can go beyond whatever blocks you have. This is painful work and has some inherent dangers. It is recommended only in extreme situations. For example, a very blocked survivor who felt an irresistible urge to cut off his penis was referred to a very senior, skilled hypnotherapist. The therapist was able to offer hospital care while the hypnosis was undertaken.

Many people are duped by the TV sitcom portrayal of hypnosis. These shows present an unsuspecting person being hypnotized, given a command, and awakened with no memory of the hypnosis taking place. In fact, you are fully awake and alert during most uses of hypnotherapy. Post-trance amnesia is uncommon and generally requires a very hypnotizable subject and a deep trance state.

Hypnosis is a structured process of relaxation designed to produce a state of dissociation. This induced state of dissociation facilitates your ability to get in touch with unconscious parts of yourself, such as feelings, awareness, or memories. While in the trance state, you can tap into your imagistic memory and retrieve repressed memories of abuse.

If you decide to use hypnosis to retrieve repressed memories, select a qualified, well-trained hypnotherapist. You may want to ask your local mental health board or state psychological association for a referral. Ask the therapist you select what his or her training is in hypnosis, how he works with repressed memories, and how much experience he has had working with sexual abuse.

Hypnotherapists are generally very creative individuals who devise their own particular styles of working with patients. It would be impossible to describe precisely what you will experience if you choose this method of memory retrieval. The basic process, however, generally involves four phases: trance induction, directed memory work, suggestion, and return.

Trance Induction

The hypnotic trance state involves selective focus of attention, relaxation, and bypassing the critical faculty of the mind. Selective focus of attention means that the hypnotherapist will ask you to focus on something, such as a mental image, an object, or the voice of the therapist. As you do this, you will be encouraged to relax your body and acquire a state of tranquility. Bypassing the critical faculty of your mind is a matter of voluntarily entering the world of imagery of the hypnotic state, so that you cease to censor your thoughts.

Directed Memory Work

After you have undergone a form of trance induction, the hypnotherapist will use some method of directed memory work. Again, the creativity and personal style of the therapist will influence how the memory retrieval will be approached. Some use very concrete questions, while others use a metaphor that focuses your unconscious on your childhood. While three possible approaches are described below, there are thousands of equally valid approaches.

Age regression is the most commonly used method of retrieving painful childhood memories with hypnosis. After trance induction, it is suggested that you are getting younger and younger. You are urged to continue to move backward in time until you get to an age that seems significant to you or that the therapist suggests you stop at. You then "enter" that age and talk about what is going on in your life at that time. If abuse occurred at that age, you rely on the unconscious to move toward revealing the trauma through imagery, feelings, and words.

Imagistic work can be done in the trance state. After trance induction, an image, dream fragment, or some other form of memory fragment is used as a focal point. The hypnotherapist acts as your guide, and you proceed just as you would in imagistic work. If you do not have a focal point to work with, some therapists suggest the image of a blank screen, and say something like,

"Watch the screen and tell me whatever you see on it." The imagistic memories are then "projected" onto the screen.

Another common metaphor is called going home. This technique involves you picturing yourself entering your childhood home. The therapist suggests something like, "You are very relaxed. You are floating down, down to the doorway of the home where you grew up. You open the door and step inside." You then describe the scenes and images that come to you as you move through the house. Again, abuse memories that are ready to be faced emerge from the unconscious.

Suggestions

Your hypnotherapist will also use suggestion to help you with your repressed memories. A trance state opens a direct link to the unconscious, and suggestions can be given that reduce or remove the unconscious blocks to memory. Suggestions that promote your healing and emotional well-being can also be given, as well as suggestions to deepen your trance state during the next session of hypnosis.

Return

The therapist will lead you in a process that helps you return to a non-trance state comfortably. The therapist may offer some sort of metaphor for reentry into a more active state. Another common approach involves counting from one to five, while telling you that you are feeling increasingly alert.

Hypnosis is very similar to imagistic work. Imagistic work is, in actuality, hypnosis without the trance induction. Imagistic work is the preferred method of memory recovery if you are not a good hypnotic subject, if you do not have access to a qualified hypnotherapist in your community, or if you have unusual fears about being hypnotized. Hypnosis is invaluable if you suffer from multiple personality disorder as a result of your abuse or if you know you were abused but have trouble accessing images through other methods.

Carol Phelps, my partner in Dallas, teaches the maxim, "You should never use hypnosis if it is the only method you have available." It is one tool in recovery of memories, but it will not give you pain-free access to your childhood. You will not get recall memories from hypnosis, and you will still have trouble believing what you remember under hypnosis.

ART THERAPY

Many survivors dismiss art therapy as a method requiring special materials, talent, or interest in art. Certainly, it can be a complex process, involving a variety of materials and approaches, but retrieving memories through art can be done as simply as journal writing. It requires nothing more than pencil and paper, a willingness to let your hands draw something, and avoiding self-criticism about your effort.

It is a technique that accesses primarily acting-out memory and imagistic memory. Acting-out memory is utilized when you allow your hand to paint or draw whatever picture it wants, without trying to control the outcome with your conscious mind. Imagistic memory is used when you translate an image that seems to be a memory fragment onto paper. Most often, you will be dealing with both forms of memory as you draw, paint, or in some other way create a visual representation of your repressed memory.

If you are interested in working with your memories using art therapy, talk to your therapist about including this method in your current work, or ask for a referral to a trained art therapist. If you decide to seek out an art therapist, interview the prospective professional carefully. Determine his or her level of expertise with sexual abuse in general and repressed memories in particular.

Memory retrieval through art can be approached in three ways. Each of these approaches provides a way of either accessing or elaborating memories through drawing or painting an image. Art is a powerful force, and you may also use other forms of creativity as part of the healing process.

Imagistic Recall Through Art

With this approach, you select an image as a focal point. You draw (or paint) the image to the best of your ability. Then you let yourself draw whatever you think happened next, avoiding censoring just as you would in imagistic recall. You may end up with a series of drawings or a single drawing that fully depicts an abuse episode. The key is to draw whatever your best guess is about what happened.

Already-Retrieved Memories

You may want to use art to create a picture of a memory that you have already retrieved previously. In putting on paper a view of the memory, you will find yourself adding details you were not aware of or had not shared with others. This technique not only retrieves more details but it also makes the memories more concrete.

Interpreting Your Artwork

You can also use your artwork much as you would your dream work to recover memories. If you enjoy drawing, painting, and artistic creation, you may find certain symbols, themes, or objects appearing regularly in your art. Interpreting these symbols, themes, or objects, just as you would in working with your dreams, may lead you to uncover repressed memories.

Bea was a survivor in group therapy who loved

drawing and always carried her sketchbook with her. When she began to share her drawings with her group, they were shocked to see the constant themes of blood, robed figures, pentagrams, Satan, and huge penises ripping through young children. Finally Bea voiced what the entire group was thinking. "I believe I was a ritual abuse victim," she said, after presenting another of her grisly drawings.

Bea worked on her memories imagistically and with hypnosis, but art remained a central method she chose to explore her feelings. She would also paint already-retrieved memories and get additional detail from her art. One day she created a painting that showed a circle of robed figures with a goat and a small child in the center.

"This is a memory. I painted it months ago, and it never bothered me. Then last week I saw it again, and all of a sudden I was really scared of it. After I stared at it for a while, I realized that this scene really happened. I painted a memory even before I knew it was a memory!"

FEELINGS WORK

Feelings work to recover memories is based on tapping into feelings memories. What you felt during your abuse is present still, and the feelings form a "feelings bridge" between the memory and now. When you encounter deeply buried emotions you have about your abuse, imagistic, body, and acting-out memory may also be activated. During the feelings work you access these other forms of memory, enabling you to get a more complete sense of the original abuse.

If you are interested in feelings work, you should do this work with a skilled professional. You are more susceptible to flashbacks during feelings work, because you break through the dissociation that normally protects you from feeling the full impact of your abuse. In a flashback you lose touch with the here and now, and you have the sense that the abuse is happening all over again. This can be frightening and dangerous for you and whoever is with you. If you do consider doing feelings work, please have a plan worked out with your therapist about what he or she will do if you experience a flashback.

Feelings work often leaves survivors with disjointed memory fragments, rather than facilitating a working through of a single abuse episode. Sorting out the resulting images can be a complex and frustrating process. If you are completely blocked about your memories, feelings work may help you access imagery or feelings memories, but it is not as effective as other approaches in helping to piece together a coherent sense of your history.

Therapists have devised innumerable ways of accessing feelings, but the process usually focuses on two basic feelings that survivors experience during sexual abuse. Rage is a primitive, animal response to brutality, which survivors must block during abuse because they are powerless. Grief is a deeply human response to loss and betrayal, which survivors must block because there is no possibility of comfort or resolution. Both of these painful feeling states can help you access the painful memories associated with them.

Rage Work

In rage work, you try to get in touch with and express the rage you feel about being abused. This rage is generally deeply buried, although it leaks out at people and obstacles in your current life, like cars on the freeway or your spouse. Experiencing it directly in relationship to your abuse involves being willing to "act as if."

The rage should be directed toward your perpetrator. Rage work can be done using a bataca, which is a large, soft bat, or anything else that can be safely used to hit with. You can also use your voice to yell. Your therapist may encourage you to begin by hitting a footstool or pillow with the bataca and yelling out as loud as you can. Sometimes you may have a sentence you want to yell, or your therapist may suggest something, such as "Get away from me," or "I hate you." Other times you may just want to make a sound, a scream of rage.

With support from your therapist, you will be encouraged to move to a deeper and deeper level of your rage. You may be encouraged to shout louder, until you sense the full power of your rage. Your therapist will closely monitor your work to see that the rage is never turned back on yourself or toward the therapist.

Grief Work

Grief is a powerful feeling experienced during and after abuse. The overwhelming sadness and longing for rescue is something every abused child feels. Touching this grief often allows repressed memory fragments to surface.

Grief work can be structured by suggesting that you curl up or lie down and begin a slow, relaxed breathing. Whenever you feel any sense of sadness, try to express a noise with the feeling. Slowly, over time, the grief will start to build.

Grief usually comes in waves, so do not be discouraged if it fades, for it will surely return. As each wave of grief is felt, let yourself moan, cry out, or sob. As the grief deepens, the related memories may also begin to surface.

The line between grief and rage is thin, and many times what starts out as grief or rage work reverses to the opposite feeling. Whichever direction you need to take is perfectly acceptable. Buried feelings take you on a journey that is not always well mapped out in advance.

After either rage or grief work, go over with your therapist what you felt, what you pictured, and what you thought about during your feelings work. This process lets you debrief the experience, as well as make explicit memory fragments of whatever you got in touch with. Make sure you have adequate support in place for any fallout you may have from the work during the next few days or week.

EMPOWERING YOURSELF

Begin by selecting one of the three journal writing techniques, or make up one on your own. Apply this technique to an image or anything else you suspect may be a memory fragment. Afterward, talk over what you wrote and your reactions to it with your therapist or support group.

Experiment with the other four techniques if your money and time permit. Select one you are interested in and investigate who is well-recommended as an expert in your community in this area. Your local rape and sexual assault center or state professional boards are places you can begin seeking a professional, but, if you know other survivors in therapy, they are your best source in your community.

Write down the pros and cons of trying a new approach, making careful note of your fears. If you wish, schedule an interview with a person you might like to work with. Inquire about his or her working style, experience, and qualifications. If you feel comfortable, share your list of concerns with this person.

CHAPTER NINE

MADE UP OR REAL?

Sarah was having trouble in her relationship with her husband. He seemed to her to be increasingly rageful, and their fighting built in intensity and frequency. He resisted seeing a marriage counselor, so Sarah felt a strong need to use her therapy hour with me to sort out her part in their marital conflicts.

When her marriage was not in turmoil, she focused on her job. Trouble with an arrogant, demanding supervisor added to her sense of stress. Her depression worsened as her efforts to sort out work and family tensions were unsuccessful.

I did not doubt that Sarah's issues in her current life were real therapeutic concerns, but I also knew the power of repressed memories to invade and disrupt even the healthiest life. Since she had not mentioned her grandfather for weeks, I asked her one day, "Where are you with the memory work you've done, Sarah?"

"I guess I've put it on the back burner for now," she answered. "The last couple of memories I worked on were so unbelievable to me. They seem so unreal now that I doubt they really happened. That made me doubt all my memories. I feel like I had some kind of attack of craziness and now it's faded."

Recent contact with her family had added to her doubts about the reality of her memories. "My father keeps talking about what a wonderful man my grandfather was.

When I told him I wondered if Grandpa abused me, he said there was no way he would ever believe anything like that because my grandpa was just too good a man. I thought that stuff just rolled off my back, but maybe it had more of an impact than I was aware of."

Sarah was facing one of the major issues in the recovery of repressed memories, the crippling disbelief that so often affects survivors. Her doubting was part of a prolonged phase in her therapy, while you may experience waves of disbelief after each memory you retrieve. Whether as a phase or waves, the disbelief is usually accompanied by massive self-hate and guilt. "How can I even think such a thing? I must really be warped," you tell yourself.

Belief versus disbelief is a valid and compelling issue. For years, therapists have tried to deal with the issue by telling clients, "The thoughts and feelings are part of your internal reality, even if the events you are picturing are imaginary. It doesn't matter if what you are experiencing really happened or not."

"It matters to me. It matters a lot!" survivors would retort. Uncovering repressed memories is no less than a search for history. Adults who were adopted often expend great energy tracing their birth parents, and this need to know is no less urgent for those with repressed memories. While some are able to turn their backs on the past, you are drawn to the search.

As you recover memories, you are faced with an uncomfortable duality. The memories you retrieve seem completely unbelievable and yet, at another level, they feel right. Your dissociation and denial clash with the emotional "fit" of the memory, setting off psychological polarization. This state of dissonance must be faced and resolved sooner or later.

Resolution does not come easily. Neither you nor your therapist want to accept a false reality as truth, for that is the very essence of madness. The need to carefully assess the truth of your memories before you assimilate them is genuine. You are seeking a balanced, appropriate sense of reality.

PITFALLS

Determining the authenticity of repressed memories is an essential undertaking, but it has a number of hidden traps for survivors. Getting caught in one of these can delay your recovery and cause you great suffering. While knowledge will not make you invulnerable, being aware of potential pitfalls in the search for reality may help you avoid some of them.

Internal Traps

The first thing to check for is if you are more concerned about your memories being made up than real. In other words, you are more worried about being "crazy," making false accusations, and causing your family all kinds of needless trouble than you are about the anguish of being abused as a young child. You are used to handling the pain in your family, and you know you will be criticized or ostracized if you talk about the abuse you remember, let alone abuse you do not remember. To protect yourself, you develop a bias against your memories being true.

You may become overconcerned about making false accusations in particular. You do not want to claim that someone abused you when that is not true, but this need for justice can take on an exaggerated importance. Having been blamed so often in your family, you can become too sensitive to fairness issues. Like so many survivors, you end up being unfair to yourself in the process.

Self-Hypnosis Masquerading as Disbelief

Autohypnotic suggestion is used during abuse to help you forget that the abuse ever happened. Repeating sentences like, "I'm making this up," or "I must be crazy," and "This isn't real," are powerful messages you gave yourself during the original abuse to cope with an unbearable situation.

Now, when the memory of that situation returns, you instinctively revert to the coping technique that helped you the first time. You try to deal with the overwhelming images and feelings by repeating the same autohypnotic sentences. You may be convinced that your disbelief is a rational questioning of the reality versus unreality of your memories, but it is partially a misguided attempt to repress the memories again.

When self-hypnosis is an issue, disbelief has a different quality from denial or a genuine effort to assess your reality. Self-hypnotic doubts that immediately follow retrieving a memory have an obsessive, desperate quality and involve one or more simple sentences you say to yourself. These simple statements occur along with your other musings about the veracity of your memories. If you feel this applies to you, or you get feedback from your therapist or friends suggesting this might be what is happening, you would do well to deemphasize or even ignore your doubts for a time. You may want to try saying affirmations about trusting your feelings to counteract the effects of your childhood messages.

Needing External Proof

You can also become too caught up in seeking external proof rather than internal relief. External proof of repressed memories is elusive, buried under the massive weight of the family's denial system, and does not help

much if you do get it. You may think you would feel
so much better if you had medical records that corroborated your memories or if someone in your family
would simply verify your stories.

Some survivors do have sisters or brothers reporting
similar repressed memories, while others have medical
records or scars that match their memories. These survivors experience the same intensity of disbelief as those
who have no external proof. The proof is rationalized
away with statements like, "My sister and I both must
be crazy," or "Maybe I broke my leg some other way
and just made this story up from books and movies."

Denise kept having images of her father raping her
when she was twelve years old. She pictured this happening during the month she stayed with him while her
mother was on her honeymoon in Europe with her new
husband. She also had a recall memory of being treated
for a venereal disease around this time.

When her childhood medical records showed she
had been diagnosed with gonorrhea the week after her
mother's return, this evidence did little to convince
Denise that her memories were accurate. She would
express disbelief, and, when confronted with the medical records, she would simply shake her head and say,
"I know. Isn't it strange?" Proof did not help Denise
with her doubts.

Proof, if it comes at all, will come after you no
longer need it. After survivors have worked assiduously
on their therapy, braved the scorn of their families, and
asserted the reality of their memories, external validation begins to arrive. This is due to the survivors letting
go of their denial, so that they accept rather than dismiss
confirming information.

Family Snares

Looking to your family to provide validation is especially risky. Abusive family members may not re-

member the abuse, but they intuitively sense that what you are inquiring about is a threat to the family system. This sense of threat often keeps them from giving what little information they do have, and they may even produce red herring stories. These are stories that may or may not be true, but their purpose is to lead you in the wrong direction.

Red herring stories either describe how the suspected perpetrator could not possibly have had access to you or extoll his or her virtues so much that you doubt yourself. Gretchen wanted to gather data from her family to check out her memories that her long-deceased uncle had abused her when she was a very young child. Her family was convincingly aghast at the suggestion that beloved Uncle Dan could have done anything so heinous. "Besides," her mother told her, "Uncle Dan died before you were even born."

Gretchen was an exceptionally determined young woman, however. She went to the county courthouse and checked his death certificate. Uncle Dan died when she was two.

Your internalized family system can also ensnare you as you do your memory work. Recovering your memories breaks the family's no-talk rule about abuse, as well as the offender's rules against remembering. When you break these longstanding rules, you feel anxious and begin to anticipate your family's reaction to what you are saying. You start mentally measuring your memories against your family's skepticism instead of your own internal reality.

Impossible Memories

Sometimes the things you remember seem like they could not possibly have happened. Either the memory contains elements that directly contradict each other, or it is too grotesque or fantastic. "I am crazy," seems like the obvious conclusion.

When a memory contains contradictory information, consider the possibility of "accordion memory." Accordion memory occurs when a young child collapses two or more memories into one, so that the composite memory has elements from more than one incident. When the retrieval process is started, the memory expands like an accordion file, exposing an entire set of related memories.

If your memories are unusually grisly or bizarre, you may be a survivor of ritual abuse. Ritual abuse is characterized by inhuman acts of physical and sexual torture, often involving groups of people performing atrocities in a pseudoceremonial setting. The ceremonies may even include human sacrifice and cannibalism. Imagery with these kinds of themes should be carefully assessed for the possibility of ritual abuse.

The torments of the Holocaust are not confined to that time in history or that country. If people could get away with mass slaughter then, they can get away with it now. Humans and the nature of evil have not changed significantly in forty years. It is plausible that sadists with a similar bent are alive and well and acting out their disease today in America.

Shawn related tales of increasing horror in her therapy. She described unbelievable acts of human sacrifice committed by a large group of neighborhood families in a small Midwestern city. Her skepticism grew with each memory. "Surely no group of people could engage in these kinds of activities without at least one of them telling?" she argued. "No group could keep that kind of secret over a long period of time."

She read a brief reference to cult abuse in a book, contacted the author, and learned from him that the kinds of behaviors she was remembering were by no means unusual. Cults use all measures of threats and mind-warping techniques to ensure silence and loyalty to the group. Shawn bravely accepted that cults are real, even though treatment and intervention were still in their infancy.

Finally Shawn realized that the cult had not kept its secret. She was telling, and probably children from the cult had been telling adults since it all began. No one was believing the survivors. What better way to keep a secret than to make sure that what is told is so crazy and awful that anyone who tells will never be heard?

Ritual abusers typically use illusions and trickery to deceive the children they are tormenting. They do so partly to make the children more malleable to the cult's influence. They have an even more chilling motive in their deception, however. Since cults thrive on the disbelief of the public, another purpose is to set up the children to appear crazy if they should try to tell someone about the abuse.

If you have memories that could not possibly have happened, first consider trickery designed to instill doubt. Ritual abusers combine sadism with intelligence. Some of the deceptions they devise are masquerading as aliens or famous people and then committing acts of abuse, staging a mock death of someone who later is clearly alive, using illusion, masks, and sleight of hand to perform "impossible" movements or acts, and inducing hallucinations with drugs and hypnosis.

Professionals who work with sexual abuse are discovering that ritual abuse, while rare, is still far more prevalent than previously suspected. An informal working group studying the phenomenon estimated that ritual abuse accounted for 7 to 10 percent of all sexual abuse survivors. If you suspect your memories have elements of ritual abuse, please consult a professional who has experience with ritual abuse for assessment, support, and help.

CLINICAL INDICATORS
OF AUTHENTICITY

Therapists who have worked extensively and sensitively with repressed memories have found that some survivors have external verification for their memories. Most commonly, siblings not in communication with each other report the same or similar memories independently to different therapists. Other times, X-rays or medical records offer supporting data. In a few instances, perpetrators have admitted to the abuse, disclosing details that they have not yet been confronted with. Whatever the source of the verification, having a pool of corroborated cases allows professionals to draw inferences about the authenticity of repressed memories that are not corroborated.

There are a few cases in which the abuse has definitely proven to be untrue. Many of these cases seem to involve people who have a longstanding history of lying, distortion, and exaggeration. These people were undoubtedly horribly abused at some point, but part of their damage is an inability to be truthful. Sometimes survivors, especially those with multiple personality disorders, include stories of abuse that they have read or overheard along with their true reports of their own abuse. It is unclear in these cases if the survivors are unaware of the distinction between their boundaries and another survivor's, if they are testing the gullibility of the therapist, or if deliberate deception is the issue.

Most therapists who work with abuse and repressed memories agree that the overwhelming majority of survivors' memories are true. This belief is based on a number of factors. The first and most important is the relatively large numbers of confirmed cases compared to the extraordinarily few cases of deception. The experience of the obvious genuineness of the survivors' stories, the logical linking of the memory to previous symptoms, and the clinical similarities among cases are just a few of the other considerations therapists take into account.

Therapists are still sorting out their clinical observations, and, as yet, no standard method exists for establishing the authenticity of repressed memories. The following is a list of the factors that are important in evaluating the credibility of repressed memories. The list is not an exhaustive one, for the complexity of the human psyche is infinite. These are currently the most common, but not the only, indicators used to clinically assess authenticity.

There is no magic number of items you need to have checked on the list, either. If only one thing on the list fits, it may be so compelling that you know the memory is real. Other times four or five items might be present, but you still may feel hesitant to conclude that what you are remembering is real because some of the pieces just do not fit yet.

Ultimately, each survivor must make his or her own judgment based on logic, feelings, and available data. If a memory fits your sense of your past, and, in the long run, you feel better for having dealt with it as real, then accept it as true. Therapists, friends, and family can all give you input, but the final judgment call is yours and no one else's.

Presence of the repressed memory syndrome. You may want to review Chapter Two for a description of the repressed memory syndrome. Going over the syndrome with your therapist will help you decide if it applies to you. Not all of the elements of the syndrome need to be present, but if most or all of them are, this is a strong indication that the repressed memories are valid.

Story matches depth of pain and symptoms. Another feature is the match between what you are remembering and the amount of pain you seem to have in your
life. A principle of treatment is that the abuse in your
life is always at least as great as the emotional pain you
suffer now. If you have a great deal of emotional distress, and the repressed memories seem to fit how much
pain you are in, then the memories are likely to be
valid.

Also notice the kinds of symptoms you suffer from
before any memories are recovered. Did you act out
sexually in a way that parallels the abuse you are now
remembering? Did you exhibit symptoms as a young
child that are commonly seen in sexually abused children? Not all abused children act out, and not all families will give this information willingly, but if
symptoms were present in your childhood, they add
substantial weight to an assessment of validity.

Brad sought therapy because he suffered from im-
potence, depression, and extreme difficulty in concen-
tration. He had virtually no memories of his childhood,
although he believed he had been profoundly emotionally neglected. He was concerned because his brother
killed himself and his sister had made a serious suicide
attempt. He also remembered crawling into closets and
hiding in nooks and crannies to avoid his mother, although he could not remember why.

Brad slowly pieced together some of his childhood
history from his surviving siblings and his own returning memories. He had been a bedwetter until he was
ten, was very withdrawn, and he had gone through a
period of elective mutism as a very young child, refusing to talk to anyone for months at a time. He had also
been caught touching his brother's penis when Brad was
four and his brother was about six months old. He
vaguely recalled the incident and said, "I remember

thinking something like, 'I guess this is how you're supposed to do it.' "

Evidence of repressed memories of abuse emerged. Brad had nightmares of a child being anally penetrated with fingers and had images of a young child being masturbated in the bathtub by a woman. Imagistic work with the scene in the tub revealed his mother teaching him how to give himself an erection. After the bath, she would give him baby oil massages that would end in her slipping her fingers into his anus.

The pain in Brad's life was compatible with the story of his memories. Emotional neglect, however severe, did not account for the kind of devastation in his life, especially coupled with two siblings' suicidal acts. The symptoms he showed also matched his story. Hiding from his mother, elective mutism, persistent bedwetting, and sexual acting-out fit with his repressed memories of sexual abuse.

The style of his acting-out was especially significant. His remembered thought of the "right" way to fondle his baby brother was consistent with his memory of his mother using a teaching rationale as a device to sexually molest him. This kind of detail directly linking the assault with the sexual acting-out is a strong indicator of authenticity.

Clinical cohesiveness of perpetrator acts. Perpetrators have certain patterns in the way they think and act. There are types of offenders, such as incest offenders, sadists, cults, pedophiles, infant abusers, female offenders, and sexual compulsives. If you seem to know or sense how a certain type of perpetrator will act, you have probably been exposed to that type of perpetrator. If you present an abuse incident that is consistent with what is known about perpetrators' behavior, it adds to the memory's validity.

Brad's description of his mother's personality and the style of her abuse conformed to clinical patterns with maternal sexual abuse perpetrators. His mother was a cold, isolated woman, and she showed indications of psychotic delusions. She was stiff and uncomfortable around children, as so many mothers who sexually abuse preschoolers are. They are quite different from male pedophiles, who come across as loving and affectionate with children. Her abuse was also staged to appear nurturing and helpful, rather than erotic in nature, which is very common with female offenders.

Supplying inconsequential detail. Survivors will occasionally offer nonessential details during memory work or in discussing their memories. The new information is offered spontaneously and usually with great certainty. They start speaking as if the images are a true memory. In the process of describing an act of oral rape, for example, they might suddenly add, "I was wearing a red dress," or "The sun was slanting through the window." If you make these kinds of disclosures, you can view them as validating your memories.

Corroborating data in family-of-origin or present life. Survivors sometimes have information that adds support to their repressed memories. Denise, the survivor who had medical records about contracting a venereal disease that confirmed her memory of being raped, is a prime example of this phenomenon. While this kind of dramatic evidence is rare, many of you have some data that link your memories with your family or current life.

Greg grew up with a terribly abusive mother. He recalled much of her violent physical and sexual abuse, but toward the end of his therapy he began to get images of her force-feeding him noxious substances. He saw her making him eat feces, Ex-lax, raw chicken parts, and even his own vomit. His therapist asked him if he had any corroborating data.

"Well, I know we were sick a lot as kids. It seemed as though one of us always had the flu. There was lots of throwing up. I guess that could be related," Greg answered after a long time in thought. "And my brother eats rotten food now. I've seen him scrape mold off luncheon meat and eat it, and once he drank a small container of machine oil."

Survivors will sometimes find old pictures showing a house, a person, or a scene that resembles something pictured in an abuse memory. Parents or other relatives may reveal trauma responses that are symptomatic of abused children. Other siblings in the family may have similar fears, imagery, or symptoms. Whatever the source, compiling an ongoing list of confirming data is at least as important as focusing on how a memory could not possibly be true.

Little evidence of sympathy-seeking behavior. Most survivors are cope-aholics, people who cope with whatever is thrown at them without reliance on others. They do not seek out sympathy for their pain and feel undeserving if it is offered. They are especially averse to sympathy from others about their repressed memories. If you have a tendency to avoid sympathy and support, it is an indication that your memories are real.

Presence of crippling disbelief. The existence of profound disbelief is an indication that memories are real. There are patterns in the disbelief such as waves of doubt immediately after a memory surfaces or after contact with unsupportive family-of-origin members. A common pattern is for survivors to get mad at anyone who does not believe their memories, but shift into disbelief when someone else does believe them.

No evidence of a florid imagination or psychosis. Some people have a tendency to embellish their stories or produce numerous, vivid images. Their minds may be flooded at times with unreal, profuse pictures, and they have little or no control over this process. If you have this type of problem, evaluate the authenticity of your memories very carefully with the help of a therapist.

Some of you are worried that you are simply responding to others' suggestions and an atmosphere of hunting for abuse. If you are highly vulnerable and easily led, it is possible that you can start looking for something that is not there. If so, you will lack the persistence to pursue the quest for repressed memories. The imagery will fade or fail to hold your attention long enough to retrieve a set of related memories.

If you have been diagnosed with a psychotic illness, in which a chemical imbalance in the brain causes you to see, hear, or believe things that are not true, assess your memories with the help of a mental health professional. A psychosis is a serious, profound illness and it can affect the authenticity of your memories. Also remember that people with psychoses are more vulnerable to abuse and more likely to be dismissed if they say they have been abused.

No internal awareness that you are lying. Unless you have a longstanding history of pathological lying, you know when you are deliberately deceiving others. It is not something you feel confused or uncertain about. If you are confused or unsure, you are not lying.

If you are deceiving yourself and others, look hard inside and face the issue squarely. Admit the deceit to all those involved, and get the help and attention you need for the problems underlying your deception. Remember, though, that these kinds of cases are very rare, so be careful not to use this issue of deceit as a way to deny your abuse.

CRITICAL MASS

You can assess the authenticity of your memories for years. Confirming and disconfirming data abound for every survivor, and sorting them out becomes overwhelming. Eventually, you may just have to decide if you think your memories are real or not.

To quote one of *Reader's Digest's* Quotable Quotes, "Some things have to be believed to be seen." You will find it helpful to decide that your memories are real for at least a year. This decision allows you to look at them with some amount of continuity, without constantly going back and forth between belief and disbelief. If the pieces do not seem to be fitting together after that time, you can then reassess the validity of the memories.

The most important step in deciding if your memories are real, however, is doing memory work. When you have retrieved enough memories, you will reach critical mass, which is a sense of the overall reality of your repressed memories. You will not get a sense of recall with your memories, but after enough memories, debriefed enough times, you will suddenly know your repressed memories are real. It is the opposite of the maxim that if you tell a lie long enough, you will believe it is real. If you talk about your repressed memories long enough, you will intuitively know they are real.

There is no fixed number of memories you will have to process before you reach your own level of critical mass. It is certainly not all your memories, but one or two will not be enough. The proportion depends on your denial system and how abused you were. Most survivors need to retrieve at least ten to twelve memories.

Not every detail of every memory will be completely accurate. We do not expect such precision from our conscious minds, and we cannot expect it from our unconscious minds, either. You may have some of the specifics wrong, but you will have the general story and most of the action as accurate as it needs to be for reality and recovery.

Once you have reached critical mass with your memories, your healing becomes easier in some ways. You are free, from the burden of doubt, at least most of the time. You know what is wrong, and when new memories surface, you process them more quickly and with greater certitude. Your path to recovery may seem just as long, but it is now a great deal straighter.

EMPOWERING YOURSELF

Go through the list of pitfalls in looking for proof. Which of these fit for you? You may want to try writing a letter from yourself from the part of you that does not believe your memories. Then write a letter to yourself from the part of you that does believe them. What do you see when you compare the two letters?

Now go over the list of clinical indicators of authenticity and apply them to yourself. Which fit and which do not? Is your denial influencing your judgment on the ones that do not seem to apply to you? Talk over your thoughts with your therapist, support group, and friends.

CHAPTER TEN

PUTTING THE PIECES TOGETHER

Once Sarah resolved much of her disbelief, she began to process more memories. She retrieved a memory of her grandfather dangling her out a second-story window after abusing her during her naptime. She remembered him choking her after an oral assault by holding her off the ground, his hands on her neck, in the dirt cellar. Another time he tried to get her to fondle his penis, and, when she resisted by pulling her hand back, he smashed the back of her hand on the kitchen table with the bottom of a thick crockery coffee cup.

Sarah was also becoming adept at recognizing when a new memory was about to emerge. She kept careful track of her nightmares and noticed when fights with her husband became charged with rage. Small cuts or scrapes would suddenly start appearing on her hands, and her depression would creep back. All these signals would alert her to the necessity of doing memory work.

She kept a list of each abusive incident she remembered, along with any significant imagery or symptoms. She decided to review this list during a session to have an overview of her progress so far. She also wanted to analyze any unfinished pieces of work.

Sarah read her list. "One. Ejaculated on me by rubbing his penis between my legs. Lowered me into the toilet hole to threaten me. Two. I cannot stand cuddling spoon-fashion, especially if I can feel breathing on my neck. Three. Washing my feet off with the wood chips in the bowl of water, then fondling me. Four. Nicking and scratching up my hands. Five. Masturbated by rubbing his penis between my legs during naptime, then dangling me out the window. Six. Making me fondle his penis and smashing my hand with a coffee cup when I resisted. Seven. Making me suck his penis in the cellar. Choked me when he came by holding me by the neck."

The first striking element about Sarah's list was the information that her grandfather's choking of her happened as he had an orgasm. Sarah's fear at that point must have been overwhelming. It gave a deeper picture of a man whose sexual pleasure was so much associated with pain and suffering.

Next she talked about all the dangling he did. He suspended her by her arm in an outhouse and out a second-story window, and he held her by her neck in the cellar. This feature of his abuse was probably intergenerational. This idiosyncratic behavior had undoubtedly been done to him in his early years.

Sarah shared what she knew of his childhood. His father had deserted the family when he was an infant. His mother remarried and appeared to despise him. He had been left out of her will completely, while his half-brothers inherited her sizable estate.

I had a sudden, clear picture of a two- or three-year-old boy being sexually abused and dangled down an outhouse hole by his mother, who hated him for his father's desertion. We will never know his full story, but at least we had a theory in the motivation behind his abuse of Sarah. Like his mother projecting her sexual needs and her hatred for her husband (and even her father?) on her baby son, he was closing the circle by projecting his sexual needs and hatred for his mother on his baby granddaughter. Sexual abuse is so often one of the strongest-held family traditions.

Sarah related a piece of data from her childhood that corroborated the memories of being dangled by one arm. According to her mother, her arm used to come out of its socket quiet easily when she was two or three. When this happened, she had to be rushed to the doctor if her arm did not pop back in spontaneously.

She suddenly realized that it was always her left arm that was the problem, and she always pictured being suspended by her left arm in her memory work. She added that she is still bothered by numbness and tingling in this arm. Her chiropractor told her that she had minor nerve damage relating to an unknown trauma to her left arm and shoulder. Another piece of the puzzle fell into place.

The second item on Sarah's list, not being able to cuddle spoon-fashion, especially with someone breathing on her neck, was an unusual phobic avoidance undoubtedly connected to a memory. As we talked she kept seeing an image of herself on his lap in the outhouse.

"I'm sitting facing outward, and he has his penis between my legs, rubbing and thrusting," she said. "I can almost feel his breath on my neck. It smells like old people and dentures and bad breath, all mixed into one. His face is near my neck and sometimes he kisses it. He smells like stale sweat, too."

She said it seemed familiar, like she knew what was going to happen next. She suddenly realized that her grandfather probably sexually abused her in the outhouse many, many times. A man who did the kinds of sick *things to a child that he did could not possibly confine his sexual assaults to only a few incidents. It is similar to assuming that an alcoholic with three DWIs and seven hangovers has probably been drunk more than ten times.*

The only item on Sarah's list unaccounted for was the symptom of accidentally cutting and nicking her hands, especially when a memory was about to surface. Her hands would get sore and slightly swollen from the cumulative effect of all the small injuries. She had tried working with her sore hands as a focal point in imagistic work, but she would only cry like a small child, without any related abuse images emerging.

Then I remembered the family story about Sarah crawling away from her grandfather through a bed of cutweeds. Cutweeds are a long grass-like weed with sharp edges along the sides that leave you with myriad tiny cuts or scrapes. I could well imagine that a number of those small nicks would make the surrounding area sore and swollen.

"What if you injure your hands as an unconscious reminder of the incident in the cutweeds?" I asked her. She got very still. "What if you were crawling away from danger, trying desperately to get away from the bad man and the pain you knew would come? Now, whenever a memory starts to return, you instinctively do what you tried to do when you were a baby. You try to escape, but you only end up with sore hands, just like back then."

Sarah's eyes filled with tears. "That seems to fit," she said. "I always feel so bad when I hurt my hands. Hearing you say that reminds me of that same feeling." She was quiet for a moment, and then said, "I wish someone could have rescued that poor baby girl."

"Someone did," I replied gently. "You saved her. She didn't have to stay there, being abused over and over. You're with her now, loving her, keeping her safe, and helping her heal."

Sarah now had a far more complete awareness of the nature and impact of her abuse. Memories, symptoms, history, and feelings were coming together to form a composite reality. This reality fit the void she sensed in her history. More memories would surface, unexplained imagery or symptoms would plague her at times, but she now had a solid foundation for future recovery.

WEAVING

Your healing is a weaving together of many strands from your life. Retrieved repressed memories, recall memories, feelings, imagery, dreams, body memories, and symptoms are woven into a comprehensive picture of the abuse you have suffered. This is both an ongoing process and something you need to specifically attend to at certain points in your recovery.

Debriefing

Weaving the pieces of your repressed memories into a coherent whole requires that you put each of the newly remembered pieces of your history into a rational framework in a process called debriefing. Debriefing means calmly and objectively talking over each repressed memory with your therapist or trusted support person. It is best done a few days or weeks after the initial memory work.

It is all too easy to retrieve a memory in a state of dissociation, feel some relief, and then put the memory away again without really facing and dealing with it. Effective debriefing helps you avoid this tendency. It allows you to assimilate the memory at both the conscious and unconscious levels.

Debriefing also gives you the opportunity to add pieces that support your original reconstruction of the abuse. Sometimes facts from your childhood suddenly make more sense and fit perfectly with the repressed memory. You never linked them with abuse because you did not have the memory back until now.

Gloria, who recalled being sexually abused by her father in adolescence, did memory recovery work one day in group therapy with an image of having been assaulted by him around the age of six. In discussing her work the following week, she threw out almost as an afterthought that this memory coincided with her history of masturbating compulsively. She told of an incident where she even masturbated at a young friend's birthday party by turning her back to the other children. "I'm sure the adults at the party must have noticed," she said. "How could they not? It must have been incredibly obvious."

Compulsive, public masturbation is a sign of sexual abuse in young children. When Gloria heard this, she felt great relief. Not only was she able to see her sexual acting-out as confirmation of her repressed memory but she also felt some of the shame from her childhood lift as she realized that her masturbation was an abused child's cry for help.

All kinds of other issues can be resolved when you debrief the memory you recovered. You can delete parts that no longer seem valid to you, or discuss your growing resistance to the memory. Adding details that you neglected to say during your memory work is possible at this time, too. Sometimes an image or sensation is far in the background during memory retrieval, so that you notice it without saying it. Debriefing lets you bring this background piece into the foreground.

Becky had worked on an abuse memory in which her father was forcing her to masturbate him when she was five. Her mother came in the room, and her father immediately slapped Becky across the face, saying, "Get away from me, you little bitch!" as if she were the one initiating the sex. Her mother came over and starting beating her in a rage.

When she was done punching Becky, she pushed her down, and Becky started to crawl away. Her mother suddenly ran over, picked her up, and held her close. She comforted her for a few minutes and put her back down. Becky remembered the scene ending in silence, as she staggered off to her bedroom.

As Becky debriefed the memory several weeks later, she added to her story, "My mother was sort of crooning a song to me when she held me. I could hear it in my head when I was doing the memory work, but it was sort of like background music. I didn't even think to mention it. It was just there, running through my head when I pictured her holding me."

She hummed the tune out loud and then felt an enormous surge of anger. "It's as if all their hypocrisy and pretend parenting and craziness are wrapped up in that pathetic little song!" she raged. "My father tricks her into thinking I was coming on to him, and my mother is sick enough to believe a five-year-old could do something like that. Then she play-acts the loving Madonna after she beats me! God, I hate them!"

The background detail of the tune her mother sang in pseudocomfort came into the foreground of her consciousness. As it did, Becky could feel the full impact of the memory. Her rage released her from a long-held fantasy that her parents were loving and protective, and she could now see them with more clarity.

Comprehensive Listing

You will also find it helpful to keep an ongoing, comprehensive list of each incident of abuse you recover to aid you in pulling together your abuse history, just as Sarah did. Include on it any imagery, dream fragments, or symptoms that might be indicative of additional repressed memories. The list serves to keep memory work you have done in a dissociated state accessible and concrete for future reference. Writing something down, or seeing it in writing later, helps you form a total picture of your repressed memories. It is a tangible reminder that you once believed this memory to be true, even if it is now shrouded in disbelief.

Include any pieces from your life that seem like clues to a possible memory, too. Err on the side of suspicion, not certainty. Your list is not an indictment of anyone, and it can always be changed. Taking time to list all your memories and unfinished pieces thus far will give you an orientation to your remaining work that is invaluable.

Closure

Closure involves assessing your memories to ensure that you have a sense of completion on each memory fragment. As you go over your comprehensive list, ask yourself, "Do I know how this memory ended?" If you do not, you may want to write out an ending for most, or all, memory fragments that do not have a conclusion.

Premature closure of a repressed memory is a very real danger for survivors. You may have a great deal of resistance in facing the reality of how an abusive incident terminates. The orgasm of the perpetrator and the way the perpetrator leaves the scene are often the two most painful aspects of an abuse incident, and, therefore, the most deeply repressed.

The offenders' narcissistic self-involvement and total

disregard for the humanity of their victim are most apparent at the point of orgasm. Then they walk out on the vulnerable child, sometimes stopping to reiterate a chilling threat, just when the child is crying out most for a loving connection and an explanation for their betrayal. It is all too tempting to just picture the abusive incident as a fade-out.

Yielding to that temptation has a price, though. Remember that the unconscious has no past or future. Everything is perceived as being in the present. When abuse is buried in the unconscious, then, the abuse never ends. It is perceived as an ongoing event, without resolution. If you do not allow yourself to face how most of your abuse incidents end, you will experience more ongoing anxiety and chaos than is healthy or necessary.

You may be reassured to know that the principle of critical mass applies here, too. You do not need to go through to the end of each incident, especially if you have hundreds of abusive episodes in your past. Be honest with yourself, do as much as you sense you need in order to feel better, and trust that your pain will tell you when enough is enough.

PRECURSORS TO NEW MEMORIES

Even if you have worked with the majority of the memories you need to assimilate, you should be aware that additional repressed memories are likely to materialize. As healing progresses, emerging memories should taper off, but even significant, powerfully traumatic memories can surface when healing seems to be the most complete. It is as if your mind senses you are strong and serene enough to deal with the really painful things now.

No definitive list of symptoms exists to tell you what to watch for with emerging memories. Signals differ from one person to the next, and each new memory can have its own unique warning signals. You need to observe your symptoms, feelings, and thoughts as each memory comes up to see if you have any particular pattern that heralds memories surfacing.

With individual uniqueness firmly in mind, there are some precursors that are fairly common. Persistent imagery is perhaps the most frequent symptom, but anxiety, inexplicable depression, nightmares, and an increase in self-abusive behaviors are not far behind. Physical injuries and unexplained pain are also typical.

Sometimes your precursor signals may be related to what you did, or wanted to do, to escape the oncoming abuse. You try to run away from the memory returning, just like you tried to run away from the abuser. Gail, for example, knows she will soon be facing another memory when she finds herself mentally calling out, "Mommy! Mommy!"

FIGURING OUT WHO DID IT

Usually survivors know the identity of their abusers early in their recovery, but sometimes this is not the case. Some of you have more trouble figuring out who abused you than you do establishing how you were abused. When this is a problem, one obvious solution is that you were abused by someone you did not know. Various people can wander through a child's life with access to the child but without a name. Babysitters, visitors, friends of grandparents, neighbors, relatives, and clandestine lovers of family members are just some of the possibilities survivors have reported.

Most of the time, however, your repressed memories indicate that the abuse happened in your own home or was too extensive for a stranger to have that kind of accessibility. The abuser has to be someone you know, and know well.

In order to determine who abused you, you will first have to let go of the urgency you have about this issue. Your recovery is not dependent on resolving this, and the answers will come to you in their own time. You may already know who it is and simply need to face what you know. Clues may come as you retrieve more and more of your memories, leading you to an inevitable conclusion. Or you may need patience, as you wait for your unconscious to do its work.

Preverbal memories. If you were preverbal when you were abused, you may not have learned the name of the person yet, even if the abuser was in your nuclear family. When the memory first surfaces, you have only fleeting, disjointed images. The name of the person is not something you can "know" and volunteer if the information comes out of a nonverbal child's mind-set.

Multiple offenders. Some of you may bounce back and forth between two or three likely possibilities. Images and clues may be confusing, too, revealing one person as the offender in one incident and someone else in another. If this is true for you, consider the obvious. Perhaps all of the people you suspect did abuse you, and the issue is not figuring out who did it but attributing which incident to which abuser.

Resistance. Resistance to your abuser being a particular individual is often a clue. In other words, the person you vehemently do not want to be the perpetrator often is the perpetrator. If you get rageful when someone suggests your father as a possibility, or adamantly assert that there is no way it could be your beloved aunt,

Renee Fredrickson, Ph.D.

watch out. Such strong feelings are sometimes more of an indication of a hated truth than a false accusation.

When resistance is deep, clues in the retrieved memories, known family history, or your internal awareness can point quite firmly to the identity of the perpetrator. That knowledge is denied because it threatens the family equilibrium or the fantasy bond you have with the alleged offender. The suspected person may be the only one who gave you any warmth when you were growing up, may appear too powerful to be accused, or may control other family members so that you would be ostracized if you revealed your suspicions.

A survivor named Rob described his ambivalence about identifying his father as his abuser. "I feel like I'm on a tightrope and can't get off. The tension is incredible, but I move from one side to the other, endlessly. I can't make up my mind, and I can't leave it alone. And the worst part is that the tightrope is attached to two parts of myself that I need to integrate."

Suggestions for resolution. If you are faced with this dilemma, first write down exactly what you would lose in your life if you decided your abuser is the person you feared it is. Then decide if you want to risk losing whatever you wrote down. Be sure to notice the cost to you in staying confused when making this decision. Is the stress worth whatever you might lose?

Be careful not to link confrontation with letting yourself know who you think your abuser is. Confrontation is an entirely separate issue. It is not always advisable or necessary, so if it is fraught with terrible anxiety for you, you will need to carefully assess whether or not to confront. That must be done at a later stage; now is not the time to decide.

Feedback from others helps, too. Ask your therapist and trusted friends who have listened to your memories who they think your abuser is. If you have an urge to argue with whomever they name, label that as resistance and avoid arguing. Remember, you are not asking them to decide. You are simply asking for their opinion.

Once you look at your external and internal information, select the person who you think is the most likely suspect. For a week or a month or a year accept that person as the one who abused you and see how that fits for you over time. When your predetermined time is up, you can reassess the situation, if you wish. Most of the time, the clues and information sort themselves out logically, with false leads and suspects dropping by the wayside over time.

GETTING THE MESSAGE

Abuse always has a spoken message and an unspoken message to the abused. Rarely is there a totally silent offender. Even if he or she is mute, the abuse carries a message in code. The abuser has something to say, the abuse is the vehicle for the message, and the child is the captive audience.

You need to find the message in your abuse. It is something you are still listening to, still believing, and still obeying. Bringing it to a conscious level allows you to respond to the message and debunk it. You break the silence your perpetrator has imposed on you.

Spoken Words

Offenders usually give two kinds of spoken messages. One is the words spoken to threaten, to keep you in silence. The second is the words spoken to shame, so that you take on the repugnance and ugliness the offender is running from. You need to dislodge these messages from your unconscious for healing to occur.

Figuring out the spoken messages is a matter of repressed memory work, once you are ready to let yourself hear. Survivors more often have spontaneous emergence of memory in this area than on any other part of their abuse. "Did he say anything to you?" is all that must be asked, and the answer is felt or heard immediately.

Tracy is a survivor who worked on abuse by her maternal grandfather and grandmother. Both of them would sexually abuse her, although each seemed to make an effort to conceal this from the other. When asked about spoken messages, Tracy said immediately, "They told me my mom was never coming back."

She said that she had a sudden, clear awareness that those words had been spoken to her. "I know I believed them, too. I thought I was going to have to live with them and be at their mercy for the rest of my life. I can feel how abandoned and frightened I felt when I heard that. The only trouble is that I don't know when—or why—they told me that."

Several weeks later, Tracy was with her mother, who began reminiscing about a vacation she and her husband had taken when Tracy was four. "I felt this charge of adrenaline the minute she mentioned their trip to New York, even though I couldn't remember anything about it," Tracy said.

"I asked her how long they were gone, and she told me about three weeks. Then I asked where I had stayed. She said. 'You stayed at Grandma's and Grandpa's, of course.' And I knew, right down to my bones, that that was when they told me that she was never coming back. And I know they did it just to be cruel and to make me frightened and dependent."

If you cannot sense or hear with your inner ear what was said during your abuse, you may have to use one of the structured memory recovery techniques to find out. Journal writing is especially useful for this. Quickly write down several sentences as "dialogue" for the offender who abused you, and then try saying them out loud to see if they fit for you.

Unspoken Messages

The unspoken message in the abuse is often more elusive and more powerfully destructive than the spoken words. The unspoken message is what the abuser wants you to know about the meaning or "reason" for your abuse. The unspoken message is always intergenerational. It is passed down from the abuser's abuser, who got it from his or her abuser, and so on.

There are some common unconscious messages shared by abusers the world over. "You're no good," "I am all-powerful," "Sex is all females are good for," "You are too sexually provocative," "You are my property," and "You are disgusting," are some of the most common. All these messages are conveyed through the nature of the abuse itself, as well as the body language and facial expressions of the abuser.

Perhaps the most graphic example of the unspoken message being delivered through the nature of the abuse is a survivor whose mother sexually abused her when she was a baby. After she was done using the child, the mother would push her face down into the wastebasket and walk away. The unspoken message is loud and clear: "You are worthless garbage." It is the same abuse message you hear when you read of dead babies being found in dumpsters, rather than buried or thrown into lakes.

Kevin finally discovered an unspoken message in his abuse that helped him form closer bonds with the people in his life. An uncle who lived with him growing up would molest him whenever his parents would go on one of their massive drinking binges. Kevin would be left without food or supervision, and his uncle would abuse him until he was hurt and exhausted.

When asked what the unspoken message from his abuse was, he replied, "No one cares about you." Then he confessed that he constantly repeats that phrase to himself, especially when he was with his lover or in his therapy group. After this disclosure, he was able to change his self-talk and open up to the pleasure of being loved.

EMPOWERING YOURSELF

If you have not already done so, write out your comprehensive list of memories, images, and clues to your abuse. Go over your list and mark the items that indicate a possible repressed memory. Also, mark the ones where closure is unclear for you. When you worked on the memory, did you work through to the point that the offender had an orgasm?

Select at least one item from your list, choose a method of memory recovery that works well for you, and come to closure with that issue. If you are unsuccessful, try a different marked item. Debrief any memories that you have not talked much about. Do as much as your energy and pain tolerance tell you is manageable for you.

If you have an issue with who your abuser is, try out the suggestions under that section. You may also want to try to assess what experiences signal you that a new memory is emerging. Keep this list somewhere accessible for easy reference over the next year.

Using the quick list technique, jot down four or five (or more) sentences that you think your abuser might have said during some of your abuse. Trust what comes to you. Try saying those sentences aloud to yourself or with someone else present, so you can hear the sound of them.

What do you think are the unspoken messages in

your abuse? Pay attention to one-liners you regularly use to shame yourself. You can also try asking the question, "What was I supposed to learn from this abuse?" In your journal, write down some statements that refute or contradict the unspoken messages you learned, and read them out loud every evening before going to sleep for one week.

CHAPTER ELEVEN

TELLING YOUR STORY

Sarah's parents were coming for a visit and she wanted to talk to them about the abuse. She had already mentioned it to her father, although just in passing, and her mother knew only what Sarah's father had told her. She was afraid to talk to them but felt ready to take the risk.

We devised a game plan for the discussion. Concerned about them ganging up on her, Sarah decided she wanted to tell them about the abuse individually, rather than as a couple. She clarified her goals in talking to them and discussed which aspects of the abuse she wanted to disclose. We also went over possible negative scenarios and came up with some strategies for dealing with them.

As the weekend drew near, Sarah grew increasingly nervous. She felt a great deal of guilt about the pain she was going to cause her mother especially and questioned the necessity of telling them about the abuse at all. I shared with her my perceptions of her mother as a woman of strength, but I stressed that she did not have to disclose to her mother if she did not want to do so. However, the decision should be made on the basis of Sarah's needs, not her mother's.

The actual disclosure went well for Sarah. Neither of her parents denied her reality, although her mother was somewhat dubious. "She told me it just didn't mesh with anything she knew about him," Sarah related. "She cried some, and then gave me a hug. That felt great, but she was horribly depressed for the rest of her visit. I felt like *she was being depressed at me, like she wanted to manip-ulate me into taking it all back. I almost did, too, but I knew I couldn't."*

In the weeks that followed, her mother sounded depressed and angry whenever Sarah talked to her on the phone. Her father, with his characteristic lack of involvement, seemed unmoved and unchanged by her story. Neither parent made any reference to the disclosure that had been so momentous to her.

Finally, she decided she had to talk to her mother about her feelings. "I don't feel a need to talk to my dad. His reaction is so typically self-involved that I don't take it personally. My mother seems mad at me and sort of punishing, and that hurts."

She called her mother and told her she needed to talk to her. "It seems like ever since I told you about Grandpa abusing me, you've been angry and distant from me. I've started to feel guilty about telling you, and I resent your reaction at the same time." She started to cry as she said, "You know, I didn't tell you to hurt you. I wanted you to know because you're my mother."

Her mother responded by saying she felt like Sarah was putting her in the position of having to choose between her deceased father and her own child. Sarah quickly said, "Choose me!" and her mother started crying. She said, "How can I think my father abused you when I don't remember him ever abusing me?"

Sarah suggested her mother might have repressed memo-ries of abuse, too, and pointed to her mother's depression as a possible symptom. Her mother became angry and defensive and flatly denied any possibility of having her own repressed memories. Sarah ended the conversation by *saying she only wanted her mother to know how she felt, not to force her into looking at her past.*

Even though the conversation with her mother did not end with a firm sense of resolution, the relationship seemed to improve after that. A few months later, Sarah remarked, "Nothing's really changed in my relationship with my parents, but, at the same time, something really important is different."

She reflected for a moment. "I think I always felt like they knew what would happen when they left me with Grandpa and just didn't care. Now my inner child knows that they didn't leave me to be hurt on purpose. I finally told, and they listened. They weren't perfect, but they did listen."

In some ways, Sarah was lucky. The abuser in her repressed memories was long dead, so her disclosure did not threaten any current relationships. Her parents were functional enough to hear her out without attacking or abandoning her. And the benefits she got from telling her story improved not only her quality of life but the quality of her relationships with her family as well.

In all likelihood, you are not as fortunate. Your family may be far more dysfunctional than Sarah's, and your abuser or abusers may still be an integral part of your life. You may even decide that your life would be in danger if you told your family members what you remembered. Disclosure is not a step to take lightly, but telling your story to someone, somewhere, is an important step in your recovery.

Your memories, which for so long have seemed unreal, gain substance each time you share them with others. Being believed and receiving the compassion of

others helps heal the wounded inner child, and dissociated feelings become accessible to you as you see the
impact your abuse history has on those who care for
you. Releasing the burden of the secret you kept even
from yourself will give you a sense of freedom that can
far outweigh any negative consequences.

In this chapter, disclosure, or telling your story,
means going over most or all of your repressed memories at one time. We are not referring to disclosing a
single memory or sharing with someone that you are a
survivor of sexual abuse. Limited disclosure has its place
in recovery, to be sure, and should be part of your
process throughout your journey. Telling all of your
story in one sitting, however, puts the whole picture
out there. The full impact of what happened can finally
be faced, giving you, and others, a new, healing perspective.

TELLING YOUR FRIENDS

It is always best to begin by telling those you expect
to be the most supportive. Your therapist, close friends,
your spouse or lover, and support groups are the people
most likely to give you the responses you need when
you tell your story. Keep in mind, though, that you are
doing this for the impact on you, not the impact on
them.

Disclosure to your therapist and loved ones is especially useful at certain critical points in your recovery. If
you feel "stuck," with no new memories coming but
no feeling of closure, telling your story can break the
impasse. It is also helpful when you have had contact
with your family-of-origin and feel yourself pulled toward their denial system, or when you are making good
progress toward eliminating self-destructive behaviors.

Lucy is a survivor with a long history of pulling out

her eyelashes and eyebrows. She worked hard in therapy on her repressed memories of abuse by her female baby-sitter and felt she had made good progress. A new medication, along with her commitment to a carefully designed behavior modification program, was helping her to break away from self-mutilating behavior.

She decided that this was a good time to disclose the story of her abuse to her husband and her dearest friend, Fran. She was aware that she might be undermining her attempt to stop her self-injury, but she felt strongly that not disclosing had the potential to be even more of a sabotage. "Now is the time for me to tell them," she said. "I need all the attention, support, and love I can get right now."

The night she told them she experienced a strong desire to start plucking her eyebrows and eyelashes. "It was an incredibly powerful drive. I asked my husband to hold me, and I promised myself I could pluck all I wanted in the morning.

"Finally, I fell asleep, and the urge was gone when I woke up. It kept coming back, though. Every time it did, I kept picturing my abuser and mentally saying, 'You're the one I want to hurt. You're the one who's ugly.' And then I would talk to my husband or call Fran. I think the worst is behind me now."

Lucy got what she needed from telling her story. Focus and concern were centered on her abuse history, not on her personal appearance. The link between her sexual abuse and the pulling out of her eyebrows and eyelashes was finally explicit, and her gains in therapy were consolidated.

Preparation

Responses to hearing a story about abuse vary widely, so be prepared to not always get what you need. If you have a death in the family, or just found out you had cancer, people generally know to offer soothing, compassionate comments. Child sexual abuse, however, is a taboo topic for everyone, and even kind, gentle people may respond inappropriately.

Prepare the person to whom you want to disclose. Let the person know what you want to talk about, and set up a mutually convenient time and place. Inform this person that telling your story will help you in your recovery. Most loving people feel flattered and are quite generous when asked to help others.

When you do meet, be as specific as possible about what you need from them. If you want them to simply listen, that is a perfectly acceptable request. Be sure to let them know what your needs are about touching. Many survivors dissociate or feel threatened when anyone initiates physical contact, and this is especially true if they are disclosing.

The person you have chosen may welcome specific information. The Guidelines for Responding to Disclosures are available to you in Appendix B. You may want to offer these twelve tips to those close to you, or use them as a starting point for a discussion on what you need in a disclosure situation.

Preparation is helpful, but do not expect perfection. Some survivors feel they were revictimized by insensitive responses when they told their story. That certainly can happen, but, at the same time, you are especially vulnerable when you disclose. In assessing the responses you get, be alert for your own heightened tendency to misinterpret, and remember that saying the wrong thing does not mean the person is an abuser or does not care about you.

Disclosure

As you approach actually sitting down to tell your story, you will not be able to predict your emotional state. Your feelings may range from terror to complete dissociation. Some survivors experience intense anxiety, while others feel perfectly fine. Most survivors feel at least some apprehension of the pain they will be revealing.

You can reveal your memories in the order in which you recovered them or in chronological order, if you are able to sort that out. It is helpful to bring a list with you to avoid blocking out significant memories, but some survivors feel this gets in the way of spontaneity. Photographs of yourself as a child can also be a compelling part of your story. You and your listener will be able to more easily picture you as young and vulnerable through the pictures.

During sharing, take the time to experience your feelings. Crying out the grief and expressing the anger within a loving relationship are very much part of the healing process. If you cannot show your feelings to the other person, at least take the time to notice them inside yourself.

How much to share is up to you. Generally, the closer you are to the person, the more details you will want to give. You do not want to be secretive or shut down, but you have a right to keep some very humiliating parts of your abuse private. You may want to only share these details of abuse with your therapist or spiritual advisor.

Disclosure reaction

Even if you dealt with your feelings as they arose during your disclosure, you will undoubtedly have some sort of a disclosure reaction, which means that feelings will come up later about having told the secret. You will not think the feelings are connected to anything in your past because these are dissociated feelings. You had dissociated feelings after you were abused, and you will have dissociated feelings after you talk about the abuse.

Disclosure reactions are sneaky. If, anytime in the

week after reviewing your abuse history, you suddenly find yourself wanting a divorce, wiping out your bank account to shop for new clothes, deciding on major plastic surgery, or refusing to get out of bed to go to work, you are probably having a disclosure reaction. Notice, but do not give in to these impulses.

Disclosure reactions are more severe if your life was threatened if you told about the abuse. Even to contemplate telling long after the abuser is dead can set off panic. After telling, the vulnerable child you once were waits anxiously for the perpetrator to return and carry out the threats.

Cal is a cult abuse survivor who decided he wanted to tell his story at a meeting of his Twelve-Step group for incest survivors. He had seen members of the cult murdered in cult "sacrifices" after being accused of betraying the cult, and as the day to disclose approached he grew more and more frightened. Normally, he knew he could trust his fellow group members, but doubts and paranoia began to creep in.

On the big day, Cal did really well. He was calm and courageous as he shared his story. His story was received with deep compassion. He passed around photographs of himself as a child, and group members pointed out that his shut-down, terrified look grew increasingly obvious over the years depicted in the photos. He found this feedback validating.

The evening after the disclosure Cal was very frightened. His fears had returned tenfold. He could not stop shaking and was quite convinced he would be murdered by the cult.

"I know my group members are not in the cult, but what if one of them knows someone who is? They might accidentally let something slip, and I could be in danger. And the janitor was cleaning the church that evening. What if he heard and is in the cult?"

He calmed down a little after talking through his

terror, but in the following weeks he remained extremely anxious. He became hypervigilant about suspected danger. Then depression settled in, along with the conviction that his life was meaningless. Suicide seemed the only valid option to him.

He finally had a breakthrough when he learned that many cults are suspected of using powerful hypnotic techniques to ensure that the children will not tell. Some even try to program children to kill themselves if they tell. He responded strongly to this information, saying it seemed to match what he was going through.

His severe disclosure reaction took several more weeks to fade, however. He needed to find out firsthand if the cult was as omnipotent as he was trained to believe it was. He was unconsciously waiting to see if they would make good on their threats to torture and kill him if he told. Only time could help him know he was safe.

Cal's reaction illustrates the difficulty ritual abuse survivors have to face in disclosing. He made a daring choice to disclose to a group, and he felt he really benefited in the long run. In general, though, if you are a survivor of a cult that is still in operation, exercise extreme caution in choosing people to hear your story.

If you do have a severe disclosure reaction, comfort and reassurance can help alleviate anxiety or self-hate. You may want to stay with someone for a few days after telling if you were violently threatened as a child. Keep reminding your adult self that your abuser does not know you told and you can now protect yourself from harm.

TELLING YOUR FAMILY

Revealing to your family-of-origin that you have uncovered repressed memories of abuse is a situation fraught with anxiety for most of you. The specter of disclosure haunts you from the very first memory you retrieved. Each returning memory is viewed in terms of eventual disclosure and weighed against your family's anticipated skepticism.

You certainly do not have to disclose to your family to recover. You can do your work, tell your story to loved ones, and keep the secret for your own protection. As a matter of fact, this method is recommended for those of you who are cult survivors or if you are from an extremely violent family. The risk to you may far outweigh any positive outcome of telling your story.

Deciding

The key in deciding whether or not to disclose is to focus on the costs and benefits to you, not your family. Keeping a secret of this magnitude from the people most directly involved should not be done in order to protect them. You have probably protected your family at your own expense far too often already.

In deciding whether or not to disclose to your family, you must realize that backlash is part of any change process. Yes, family members will experience pain and anger if you tell. Yes, in all likelihood, they will try to discredit or punish you for telling. And, yes, you are strong enough to survive and thrive in spite of their reaction, if you feel disclosure is in your best interest.

Once you accept the inevitability of backlash, you can begin to assess how your family will attempt to punish you if you tell. In general, the more dysfunctional the family, the more inappropriate their response to disclosure. Never expect a sane response from an insane system.

Your family's relationship to your abuser is also critical in determining their reaction. If your abuser is long dead or much despised, the family will not feel threatened by disclosure. Peripheral aunts, uncles, and cousins are also not very central to family functioning. Accusations of parents, grandparents, or older siblings strike at the core of the family, of course, and are met with vehement denial and defensiveness.

Family members may not actually be close to whomever you confront. Instead, they often have a fantasy bond with the abuser. They perceive him or her through the filter of their own needs, seeing qualities of character that are not really there. Fantasy bonds are common in incestuous families, and they are always viciously defended. If you suspect your family has a fantasy bond with your abuser, be prepared for a pitched battle if you do decide to confront.

Gwen is an intelligent, mature woman in a high-powered career who had been sexually abused by her maternal grandfather. Her memories of him abusing her began surfacing when her first grandchild was born. She worked hard in her therapy and finally came to the point where she wanted to disclose to her family.

Her mother reacted in horror to Gwen's story. "My daddy could not do such a thing!" she screamed at her daughter. "He was a wonderful father, a man who gave everything to his family. How dare you say such filthy things about him!"

Gwen felt shocked and betrayed by her mother's reaction. She aid, "Everyone knows he was a drunk and a womanizer. He even had two illegitimate children by another woman in town. My mother never spoke his name as far as I can remember all the while I was growing up. Now she's acting like he should be ordained for sainthood. What's wrong?"

Gwen learned that her mother had a fantasy bond with her father. Her mother covered over years of pain and abuse with an idealized picture of the father she really wanted. She may have gotten some warmth and acceptance from her father that she never got from her mother. Every child needs at least one parent who loves them, even if the love is a fantasy.

Once Gwen understood her mother's dilemma, she was able to protect herself appropriately at the next attack. She stood her ground about the abuse by him but no longer expected her mother to join her in her anger. Her mother never wavered in her loyalty to her dead father.

The kinds of punishment families mete out when you break the no-talk rule about abuse fall on a continuum. Healthier families will react with shock and sadness to hear of your suffering. Less healthy families are disbelieving, labeling you as crazy or living in a fantasy world. Families in total denial will ostracize or disinherit the survivor, and extremely pathological families threaten violence or death.

You can probably predict fairly accurately what your family will threaten to do if you tell. You may be less accurate about what they actually will do to you. You see them as more powerful than they really are because they were all powerful when you were small. Whatever you picture them doing will be inflated by your childhood sense of vulnerability.

Once you have sorted out what might happen, you must now weigh the risks and benefits to you. Make this a real decision. Too many survivors never get past their fear of their family to let themselves have an honest decision. They say to themselves, "I could never tell my family!" Work toward saying, "I really could tell my family! Now, do I want to?"

Disclosure

Once you make the decision to go ahead, the actual disclosure is an empowering experience. Telling the people in your family how you were hurt is the most expedient form of healing. Now you are finally free to speak the truth.

First share your story with family members who are most likely to be supportive. If others in your family are in recovery, were in the victim role growing up, or seem sympathetic to abuse issues, they should be your first choice. The suggestions for telling your friends can be applied in this situation, although you may have to expect less support from family than you would from friends.

You want to at least let them know who abused you, what form the abuse took, and how long it went on. If it is safe enough, you will find it helpful to talk specifically about the most traumatic incidents. The more kindness in your family, the more details you can reveal.

Avoid being tentative about your repressed memories. Do not just tell them; express them as truth. If months or years down the road, you find you are mistaken about details, you can always apologize and set the record straight. Doubts that you have should be fairly resolved before you disclose to your family.

You cannot wait until you are doubt-free to disclose to your family. This may never happen, and, if it does, it will happen after you disclose to your family, not before. You cannot fully face and resolve your own doubts until you have faced and resolved your family's reactions to your memories. You have internalized your family's denial about your abuse as a young child, and telling your family as an adult allows you to externalize that denial. You can then begin to separate your doubts from their denial.

You can disclose in a therapy session if that fits for you and if your therapist is comfortable with the idea. Ask your family members to come to help you in your recovery, not to work on relationships in the family. Tell your family the purpose of the session when you first ask them to come, even if you expect them to balk.

People are more likely to come to a war than an ambush.

Drawing up a list of the abuse issues you want to cover and going over it with your therapist is an excellent way to prepare for your session. Then bring your list to your session, and refer to it at least once to make sure you cover what you want to cover. You are very susceptible to blocking out significant incidents you want to cover in such a highly charged atmosphere, and your list will help prevent that.

Let yourself experience your feelings in your family session, too. This does not mean you should do rage work in your session. You have hopefully done much of that prior to coming to this point. It does mean that when your feelings surface about what you are saying, it is okay to let them show.

Your family probably will not give you what you need, but we do not let ourselves show our emotions only to get what we want. Feelings give us depth and clarity in our experience of the world. Showing your pain and anger about what happened to you is part of your healing.

Denials

The part you are probably dreading is how to handle your family's denial of your repressed memories. Begin by trusting that you will know what to say to take care of yourself. You do not have to counter every argument or attack they make. You only have to assert your reality, even if you are the only one who perceives it.

It is helpful to role-play in advance what some of your family's responses might be. Expect and prepare for the worst, but be prepared for the unexpected. Your family will invariably come up with some response that you did not anticipate.

If the perpetrator is in your family-of-origin and at-

tends your session, he or she most likely will deny that
the abuse ever happened. Sometimes there is outrage,
but usually the abuser will be cool and collected, simply
stating that there is no truth to what you are saying.
This calm attitude can be very influential to other family
members who do not want to believe you in the first
place.

Do not retreat. You may want to suggest that the
abuser has repressed all memory of the abuse. If you
know of other abuse perpetrated by this person, bring
it up, by all means, but do not get into a reality war
with an abuser. A suggested response might be to look
him or her in the eye and say, "You and I both know
that what I am saying is true."

Betty confronted her father in a family session. She
was strong and courageous, but he was very persuasive
in his protestations of innocence. Finally she said to
him, "You have forgotten what you did, you were too
drunk to remember, or you're trying to con me."

She was watching her father closely as she spoke.
When she said the phrase, "or you're trying to con me,"
he turned a bright, embarrassing red. He seemed unaware of his body's betrayal, but his subsequent denials
lacked force. The family could not have articulated what
changed, but every one of them responded at some level
to his nonverbal cue.

These covert signals that substantiate your memories happen often in family sessions. They may be nonverbal signals, as in Betty's case, or a turn of the phrase,
or a sudden silence. Outside observers are more likely
to notice these things at a conscious level than family
members, so your therapist or support people who are
present for the session can be particularly helpful.

Another common form of denial is to accuse you of
getting your facts wrong. Family members, especially
parents, jump on what they perceive as discrepancies.
"Uncle Hal didn't have a mustache!" "We didn't live in

that house when you were three!" You can end up feeling disoriented and discredited with this ploy.

Remember that it is just as likely that your family's facts are wrong as it is that yours are. After all, they have an enormous investment in misperceiving the past and maintaining the status quo. You may want to point this out, but, again, it is best to avoid a reality war. Simply state something like, "I may have some of the pieces in the wrong place, or some memories blended together, but I know that the abuse happened basically the way I am describing it."

If your family could respond the way you wanted, you would not have had to repress the memory in the first place. As you handle their denials, you are given an opportunity to see the family dysfunction more clearly. You do not have to convert them; you only have to free yourself. If necessary, you can tell your story and agree to disagree.

Afterward

A colleague, Jacquie Trudeau, explains that when you break a family rule, you feel terrified contemplating it, wonderful while you are doing it, and guilt-ridden afterward. You break one of the biggest rules in your family when you talk about what you are not supposed to even remember in a family disclosure session. Afterward the guilt will set in.

Typical post-session guilt can be devastating. "How could I have put Mom through all that? What if I'm wrong? Here I am, accusing someone of something that could be just a fantasy of mine. Maybe I'd better call them and tell them I may be mistaken."

After disclosing you need the support of your friends who know your story. Debrief the session with them, and talk about how you are reacting. Feedback and time will help you get the session in proper perspective. It is unlikely that you have made a major mistake, or that you are an awful person for saying what you needed to say, but you will have to hear this encouragement from someone besides yourself.

The pain of confronting your family is equal to the strength you gain from doing it. You will begin to feel some of this strength flowing into your life several months after a disclosure session. This is a long time to wait, but it will take you that long to process the aftermath of such an important step in your life. You need time to lay your guilt to rest, deal with the family backlash, and test whether your abuser's threats will come true.

EMPOWERING YOURSELF

If your therapist is willing, set aside one of your sessions in therapy to tell your story from start to finish. Include all the memories you have recovered so far. Then select a friend or support group to disclose to, if you wish. Take your time with this step. Several months is not too long to handle this kind of major undertaking.

Review Chapter Four on the family, and go over the roles your family members take in response to abuse. Decide if you can disclose to one of them, and then meet to tell your story. Do *not* do this disclosure if you are a cult survivor unless you and your therapist feel strongly that you are safe in disclosing. Keep a journal of your reactions before, during, and after disclosing to a family member. Use this information to help you decide if you want to tell other members of your family. Let several people in on your decision-making process, so that you get as much feedback as possible.

Write disclosure letters to all your family members without mailing them. Again, keep a journal of your reactions to this process. Let yourself imagine how you would feel if you did mail them. What punishment can you expect?

Ask yourself how you would feel if you never told your family. Write down your reactions to this question. Ask yourself how you would feel if you did disclose, and write down your reactions to this question.

CHAPTER TWELVE

HEALING

Sarah's healing first became apparent in her dreams. One day she recounted a dream in which she was terminally ill. Her mother was with her in a barren room, and they where both scared about what was in store for her. A door opened and a very respectable-looking doctor strode in.

He examined Sarah and informed her that he could treat her. He was very clinical, detached, and completely unwilling to have a personal relationship with her. He did, however, assure her that she would not die of her disease.

Sarah was put off by the personality of the doctor, but his role in her dream was positive. "This is the first time a healer has appeared in your dream world, Sarah," I explained. "He may be cold and supercilious, but that is exactly the kind of relationship you have with your inner child sometimes.

"Your mother couldn't save you, but your unconscious sees someone else, some other part of you, that can help. Your healer will be back, although probably not as the same character. I'll bet he or she will be warmer and more personally involved with you when you develop more compassion for yourself."

Several weeks later, Sarah had one of her psychopath dreams. She called them that because they always had an inhumane psychopathic killer in them who inexorably stalked Sarah's dream self to rape or murder her. This dream had the same theme, but a woman came in the house near the end of the dream.

Sarah said, "Just like in my woodchopper dream, I knew I was as good as dead. This time, though, there was a baby in the house, and I sensed the killer would not touch her. At the very end of the dream, this woman comes in the door, finds the baby and me hiding in the closet, and risks her life to lead us to safety."

The healer was now a rescuer, and she was strong and caring besides. This situation showed substantial progress from the impersonal doctor who could help but did not care. And, finally, her psychopath dream ended with something other than the certainty of her assault or death.

The immunity of the baby from the crazed killer was another positive development in Sarah's dream life. Before this time, the psychopath had no limits on his capacity for atrocity. Sarah's unconscious was finally beginning to recognize that her baby self had survived.

She had another psychopath dream a short time later. She was walking through beautiful countryside when she spotted a man working in a garden. She approached him and felt an instant sexual attraction to him, but when she saw his eyes shift around to see if they were alone, she knew that he was a rapist.

He captured her and put her in a metal shed. She knew his plan was to keep her prisoner and sexually assault her at his whim. She described the trapped, helpless feeling that was such a familiar theme in these dreams and in her abuse.

This time the dream did not fade out with her being trapped. Sarah began to access the metal shed for avenues of escape. She decided her best chance was to dig out where the dirt floor met the wall. The dream ended with her having scooped out a three-foot hole, nearly big enough for her to squeeze under.

This dream represented incredible progress. Sarah's fleeting sexual attraction to the psychopath indicated she was developing a relationship with her internalized tormentor and was reclaiming her sexuality from her grandfather. She had moved from a symbolic mother who could do nothing to prevent her daughter's death, to a woman hero figure saving her and a baby, and, finally, to rescuing herself from the clutches of a madman. Saving herself empowered the survivor in Sarah.

After this series of dreams, Sarah really blossomed. Her relationship with her husband stabilized. She took on new challenges at work, and, after a series of successes, decided to quit her job and start her own business. Her energy began to focus more on the present and less on the past.

Sarah continued her work in therapy for over a year after this time. Several new memories emerged, but she dealt with them with far less emotional turmoil than before. Her panic attacks were a thing of the past, and her other symptoms began to fade.

She was most delighted about the absence of even a hint of depression. "I never really knew how depressed I was until it lifted," she explained. "I had black moods that I called depression, but I must have been depressed all the time. It was so constant that I never saw it as abnormal. I didn't know there was any other way to feel.

"It's wonderful to have that aura of grimness gone. Things still get painful and tense in my life, but I have a solid sense of serenity and security I never had before. I can appreciate my husband and daughter now because I'm present in a way I wasn't before. I really feel blessed."

Sarah's journey was drawing to an end. The traumatic events that shaped her life were no longer inaccessible to her. They had been sought out, faced, and integrated into her view of herself. What was forgotten was now remembered, and the past could be allowed to fade.

You may feel hopeless at times, but you, too, will come to a point where the past begins to let go of its grip on you. Post-traumatic stress does fade with time, especially if you debrief the memories and permit yourself to have the feelings. Whatever stage of the journey you are at with your repressed memories, you will reach a point when this happens for you.

This is not a promise for everlasting happiness once you have dealt with your abuse history. Your pain will be lessened, not removed. The depth of your pain will not change, but how often you feel it will. On our deathbeds we will still be able to weep bitter tears about the pain in our childhoods, but we may not have even thought about it for years.

THE STAGES OF HEALING

Survivors seem to go through distinct stages in the healing process. Not everyone goes through each stage in the same way, or even in the same order. How memories surface is too individualistic to fit a linear description, and human beings are too complex to ever be perfectly categorized. You will do best to view the stages as general guideposts to describe common experiences for survivors.

Chaos

Your first encounter with repressed memories is one of confusion and chaos. It is the period of time when incomplete memory fragments are surfacing. Nightmares are common, as is a high level of general anxiety. You may be in denial about your abuse, which clouds the picture even more. You may suspect, or even know, that you were abused, but you still find yourself asking, "What is happening to me?"

Shock, fear, and horror are the predominant feelings during this stage of recovery. "It just can't be true!" you think. You are afraid of what you will have to see and feel in order to sort out your abuse history. One survivor described this phase effectively. "It's like my unconscious is taking the rest of me on a roller-coaster ride that I know is going to last at least a couple of years. All I can do is hang on, try not to fall off, and scream."

Breakthrough

The breakthrough stage comes after you take your first serious look at your repressed memories. You have recovered at least one major memory and followed it through to get a complete picture of what happened. You accept the idea that you have been abused and have repressed it.

A sense of relief often characterizes the breakthrough stage. After doing memory work, or having a major memory return spontaneously, you feel like you have finally faced the enemy and survived. You have answered the question of what is happening to you that so frightened you in the chaos stage.

At this point, many survivors also feel like they are through having memories surface. The bare outline of their abuse history is all they have, but because it is newly discovered, they falsely assume that is all they will have to experience. It does not occur to them that if their abuser went so far as to do the ugly things they have now remembered, he or she must have done much more.

Sue discovered she had repressed memories of abuse. She had dreams, flashes, and body memories that led her to believe her mother had sexually abused her. Working on her own, she had pieced together two complete memories.

In one, her drunken mother came into the bathroom when Sue, who was about nine, was bathing. Her mother got in the tub with her and pushed her breasts at Sue's face, cajoling her to fondle and suckle. Sue refused, and her mother started slapping and pinching her until Sue gave in.

The second memory was of her mother stripping her clothes off and getting into bed with her in the middle of the night. Sue thought she was younger in this incident, guessing her age at seven. Her mother pushed Sue's head down and talked softly as she maneuvered Sue into position to perform oral sex.

Sue felt a sense of triumph about figuring out the dark secret of her past. "Now I know what's been lurking in the background of my life, dragging me down. I have tremendous pain about this abuse, but I plan to confront my mother and get on with my life. I'm not going to let this take anymore out of me."

Sue's elation was temporary. The abuse she described was so profoundly pathological that it was unlikely that these were the only two incidents. An abuser who was this predatory would certainly not have enough impulse control to engage in two wholesale sexual assaults of her daughter and then quit. Sue would undoubtedly have to face more of her past than she currently planned.

Perseverance

The full impact of the depth and nature of the re-pressed abuse memories begins to hit. Memory fragments surface faster than you feel able to deal with them, and you alternate between periods of dissociation and frightening clarity about how bad things were for you growing up. Full-blown delayed post-traumatic stress disorder appears. (If you think you might be at this stage, you may want to review the PTSD symptoms in Appendix B.)

The symptoms that seemed so confusing to you during the chaos stage are now grimly familiar, and you may tend to isolate. Nightmares still occur, and at the same time, you feel less deserving of sympathy. You are concerned that you are exhausting your support system. Flashes of imagery still strike, but you may neglect to tell your therapist, group, or friends about some of them. You have become so acclimated to the process of memories intruding that you simply endure.

If you tend to have flashbacks, they are likely to occur at this stage. Never deal with flashbacks without professional help. You may need medication or hospitalization if the flashbacks are triggered in places that are unsafe for you, such as at work or while driving. Some of you are aware during a flashback that what you are picturing is a memory superimposed on your current reality, and that gives you some control. If that is true, you will be able to learn other ways to increase your control.

Depression either sets in or worsens. It is hard to get up in the morning, and some of you might be afraid to sleep at night because your nightmares are so terrifying and relentless. Above all, you feel hopeless. Your life seems hopeless, and the possibility of ever getting your memories back seems hopeless. You are quite certain you will never recover. Everything seems grim and colorless, and you cannot remember ever feeling any other way. You may want to ask your therapist or family doctor for a referral to a psychiatrist to see if medication will help your depression.

Your emotional life is likely to be very painful during this phase of recovery. The shame that accompanied the original abuse surfaces when the memory does. Survivors experience feeling ugly, dirty, and fundamentally flawed in some nameless way. Suppressed rage emerges, too, but it is usually directed at yourself or some aspect of your life which, unknown to you, was affected by the abuse.

The hurt and sadness stay underground, worsening the depression. To feel these emotions requires compassion for oneself, which is usually inaccessible to the survivor at this stage. You view the inner abused child with the same disdain and contempt that the abuser projected onto you. You cannot yet cry for the child that was you.

Sometimes physical illness or injury incapacitates survivors during the endurance stage of healing. Abuse stresses the body terribly, and recovering memories re-creates that stress to a certain extent. Your immune system may not function as well, and your body becomes vulnerable to disease. You may be dissociated much of the time and, therefore, not as able to prevent accidents.

You may feel like you are simply enduring, but what you are really doing at this stage is persevering. You need to keep doing your memory work, hold your life together as best as you can, and weather the feelings and misfortunes that come your way. Relate what is happening to you and what you are feeling to your repressed memories whenever you can, so that the links between your conscious life and unconscious memories become explicit.

In this stage of recovery you feel the least deserving

of love and attention, but it is the stage in which you need the most help. Ask for and take all help and encouragement you can, and then ask for a little more. Now is the time to join with others in the world to let them help with your suffering, just as you help with theirs.

Resolution

Finally, the pressure begins to ease as you enter the resolution stage. You now believe your memories are real, although you may have occasional moments of doubt even now. You have pieced together a fairly complete sense of your repressed memories and accept them as part of you. You have told enough friends that your abuse history seems talked through, and you have told your family or are considering confronting them about your memories.

Certainly the best part of this stage is that your PTSD symptoms will fade. Nothing dramatic happens to mark this, but, as you look back over a several-month span, you notice that your nightmares have vanished, depression has lifted, and you have been experiencing less pain. Avoidances and attractions to things that remind you of your abuse may still be with you, for they are often the last PTSD symptoms to leave. Still, the intensity behind your reactions should diminish.

Healing dreams may begin to appear. Your rapist may turn into your therapist, or you may start to dream of small worms instead of large snakes. Themes in your dreams will reflect a growing ability to avoid danger or extricate yourself from it. The figure of a healer, teacher, or rescuer may materialize.

Grieving is the emotional work of this stage. The sadness of the hurt child will finally be accessible to you. You may feel a great sense of loss that encompasses the loss of your childhood, the loss of time spent dealing with abuse, and the loss of your family as you knew it. As you cry out your grief, rage accompanies it. You feel outraged that your abuser did this to you, and this time it is directed at the perpetrator, not at yourself.

You will have to work at some sort of resolution with your family-of-origin at this stage of healing, which does not necessarily mean that your family will accept your memories and you with open arms. Some of you may have to reach resolution by recognizing that your family is too toxic for you to be around and grieve the loss you feel. Others of you will learn to set limits on interactions with family, structure ways to protect yourself, or maintain your belief in your memories in the face of family denial.

You will probably still have memories returning, even at this stage. You will be quicker to identify the signals that a memory is emerging, and the memory work itself causes far less disruption in your emotional life than before. It is a bit like finishing a jigsaw puzzle. The struggle to find the first few pieces and the labor of putting together the seemingly endless puzzle are replaced at the end with the more methodical routine of filling in the final pieces.

Repressed memories may return off and on for many years, or even for the remainder of your life. You now have the skills and support system to handle returning memories without the extensive shock and pain you felt when you first discovered you had repressed memories. You may need more in-depth support and therapy if you discover a new, deeper level of abuse at a later time, however.

Amy found she had to return to therapy to integrate her present life with newly emerging memories. She had left a therapy group after spending three years dealing with repressed memories of her mother sexually abusing her throughout her childhood. Her father had played a passive, neglectful role in the abuse, but no memories surfaced of him abusing her until three years after she left group.

Memories of her father began to emerge when Amy decided to start dating again. Until then, she had led a quiet, somewhat isolated life and avoided sexual relationships because of the tension they produced. When she began to actively pursue a loving relationship, she was flooded with memories of both her parents abusing her.

The newly returned memories made it clear that the level of abuse she had suffered was far greater than her first time through therapy had exposed. She now remembered her mother holding her down while her father raped her and both of them assaulting her at the same time. In her teenage years, they had forced her into group sex with neighbors and friends of the family. Clearly the abuse was much more extensive than encapsulated incest with her mother.

Amy went through all the stages of healing again. Only her strong determination and her desire to resolve this situation so she would be free to have a loving relationship kept her going through the next four years of therapy. Many times she felt so damaged that she feared she would never have a normal life. She prevailed and reached her goals in therapy and in her personal life.

Empowerment

Empowerment is something that happens throughout your healing, as courage and success in facing your memories build your self-esteem. It is also a process that persists past the point of resolution and continues for months and years afterward. Some of the strength you get from taking on your buried memories does not show up in your life until long after resolution has been achieved.

Your recovery from abuse is like recovering from a severe illness that required you to have an operation.

The operation was painful but successful. Nonetheless, your recovery is slow and requires a great deal of patience. The stitches heal, the pain subsides, and you can resume your normal activities. You consider yourself recovered.

For the next year, though, you tire easily and need more sleep than usual. You may be more prone to minor viruses because your immune system was so stressed. You can still feel an occasional ache or twinge at the site of your operation if you overdo.

Finally, after a year or so, your strength returns. Your recovery is truly complete. You feel healthy and vital, better than you have felt in a long time. You bring new energy to the tasks and joys in your life, and you may even feel ready to strike out in some new directions.

Empowerment reaches its peak long after resolution, just as full recovery from an operation becomes realized long after the stitches heal. The energy to take on old, stubborn problems of yours and reach out for new adventures will continue to build for a long time after you feel you have reached some kind of peace with your repressed memories. You will grow in spiritual, physical, and emotional strength for years to come.

FACTORS AFFECTING HEALING

Healing is influenced by a number of factors. Becoming familiar with them will enable you to assess the strengths and weaknesses you bring to your healing. At the same time, everyone's journey is unique. Spiritual and life forces come together to influence the nature and duration of each survivor's recovery. The only true constant is that recovery does take place.

Survivors too often think that the length of their healing time is a reflection on them, which is simply not true. You can do a few things to influence your healing process, but much of it is beyond your control. To quote an old Twelve-Step saying, "It takes as long as it takes." One year is more than enough time, and ten years is not too long. Be loving to yourself about this, for abuse damage heals slowly.

Extent of Abuse

How long it takes for you to heal is determined largely by how much abuse was perpetrated on you. If you were subjected to years of the most horrible torture, it will generally take you longer than someone like Sarah. Although her abuse was severe, her abuser did not live with her on a daily basis and died when she was four. How long a broken leg takes to heal depends to a great extent on how badly shattered it was in the first place.

You may have been so terribly frightened and tormented that you have a multiple personality disorder. People with multiple personality disorder use memory repression as part of their daily survival. They develop the ability to produce amnesia in themselves so they do not have to remember any of the abuse. Eventually, those parts of themselves develop into separate personalities that come forward to handle whatever they are supposed to handle. When the trauma is over, the memory of the event and the part of the person that handled it is repressed again.

Janelle, a shy, gentle soul, had been brutally abused by her sadistic father and developed a multiple personality disorder. Her abuse memories were held by various personalities, or parts of herself, that experienced the abuse and kept it hidden from Janelle so the whole of her could survive. In therapy, each of these personalities was identified and each shared what it remembered of the other personalities.

Working with Janelle was difficult, however. Before she did memory work, she would often strike a completely rigid pose. She would remain totally still, and, if spoken to, she would whisper, "Shh." Only her eyes would move, darting frantically around the room. Sometimes these periods of silent stillness would last for most of the therapy hour. If anyone spoke to her, she would whisper, "I'm listening. Shh. He might be coming."

Janelle's stillness was actually another personality. Her name was The Listener. The Listener had the job of listening carefully for the approach of Janelle's father, so the others would have warning. Nearly every abusive episode was preceded by The Listener doing her sentry job, and so every attempt to recover a memory would begin the same way.

If you have a multiple personality disorder, you may go through a longer healing process than someone who does not. This is not because having multiple personalities is a worse problem, but because more severe abuse causes multiple personality disorder. Severe abuse usually takes longer to recover from than less severe abuse.

Memory Recovery Work

Memory recovery work in the basic healing force for repressed abuse memories. The bulk of your repressed memories need to be identified, retrieved, and debriefed for healing to occur. The more you have undergone, the more memories you will need to confront in proportion to your abuse.

How diligently you do memory recovery work is one factor that is at least partially under your control. The more often you do the work, the quicker your healing. Facing your memories is painful and, therefore, easy to avoid, but it is an extremely important factor in the length of the healing process.

Denial

Denial also has a major impact on the length of recovery. Survivors with very little denial can move through therapy fairly quickly, even if their abuse was massive. On the other hand, some survivors struggle for years simply to acknowledge that they were abused. They then go through additional long periods of denial, alternating with brief periods of dealing with their memories. Their path to recovery is twisting and arduous.

You have some control over your denial. If you have a strong denial system, you can work on dismantling it with a skilled therapist. Learn to recognize behavioral cues and self-talk that indicate you are in a denial phase. Once you recognize you are in denial, talk it out in therapy and with friends who are supportive of your recovery. Avoid talking to people who are in their own denial and therefore enable yours. All these measures can help speed your recovery.

Nurturance

Having had some form of nurturing as a child helps, too. A parent, a devoted aunt or grandfather, or even a neighbor or teacher who loved you is a powerful influence even into your adulthood. For those of you who were totally abandoned and rejected as children, you can compensate by surrounding yourself now with loving supporting people. It is especially important to be around people who believe your repressed memories are real.

Your Life Spirit

The final factor affecting healing is you. The unique spirit that is you brings to your process a mysterious, immutable force that profoundly influences your recovery. Your determination, strength, humor, love, gentleness, and compassion all influence what happens to you and what happens around you. Who you are can speed your own, and others, healing.

EMPOWERING YOURSELF

Use this chapter to give yourself hope. You may not be where you wish you were in your healing, but you probably feel stronger than when you first began. Healing from repressed memories, and abuse in general, is a process that leaves you wiser and more beautiful than you were before.

Wherever you are in your healing, you deserve to be proud of your strength and courage. Let the shame of the past stay with the offender and the people who let you down. You are not worthless because someone abused you.

On display in the Freer Museum in Washington, D.C., are ancient Zen ceremonial bowls renowned for their delicate beauty and fine craftsmanship. Over generations of use these lovely porcelain bowls became cracked and chipped, and some had whole pieces missing. Rather than being discarded or devalued because of the damage, the porcelain was repaired with gold. The gold adds strength, beauty, and value to the bowls, and the sacred bowls are marvelously enhanced by the repair process.

So it is with survivors. You were damaged as you grew up, and the more abusively you were handled, the greater the damage. When you undertake to repair this damage, you replace bitterness and sadness with understanding and healing. You become stronger and more resilient when change comes. You grow kinder to yourself and more compassionate toward those you love. You, like the sacred bowls, are enhanced rather than diminished by the repair process.

APPENDIX A

PTSD SYMPTOM LIST

The following list describes the most common symptoms of PTSD. You may want to go through it, jotting down in your journal those that apply to you. Please remember that this list is not an accurate way to decide if you have PTSD. That can only be done with the help of a qualified professional.

PTSD Symptoms

A. A traumatic event is reexperienced in at least one of the following ways:

1. Distressing memories of the event, including sudden flashes of scenes of the abuse that intrude

at unexpected and unwelcome times, as well as enduring haunting memories of the abuse.

2. Recurrent distressing dreams about the event. For sexual abuse survivors, this includes nightmares that are about sexual abuse or menacing perpetrators.

3. Suddenly acting or feeling as if the event were happening now. Includes a sense of reliving the event, seeing an image of the event as if it were real, and flashback episodes, even those that occur upon awakening or when intoxicated.

4. Intense distress when exposed to events that symbolize or resemble some part of the trauma, including anniversaries of the trauma. For example, many sexual abuse survivors have very negative feelings whenever sex is initiated because it reminds them of the sexual abuse. Survivors also often react to seemingly inconsequential objects or events because these things remind them of the abuse. One woman reported a strong aversion to the odor of coffee because she was abused by her brother in the morning while her mother was busy brewing the coffee.

B. Avoidance of things that remind one of the trauma, or numbing of general responsiveness, indicated by:

1. Efforts to avoid thoughts or feelings of the trauma, including thinking about, remembering, or dealing with any of the feelings about the sexual abuse. Needless to say, this symptom can be a serious impediment to any therapy that focuses on sexual abuse.

2. Efforts to avoid activities or situations that remind one of the trauma. Many survivors are told they suffer from a disorder or desire because

they have little desire for or interest in sex. In fact, they are avoiding an activity, sex, that reminds them of their abuse. Survivors will also avoid baths if they were abused in the bathtub, dentists if they were orally abused, or pelvic exams if the exposure reminds them of their abuse.

3. Amnesia for an important part of the trauma. Notice that this symptom does *not* apply to survivors who have complete amnesia with no memory at all of their abuse.

4. Markedly diminished interest in significant activities, like work, relationships, or recreation.

5. Feelings of detachment or estrangement from others.

6. Restricted range of feelings, including feeling only rage, pain, or numbness, as well as the absence of loving feelings, joy, or closeness.

7. Sense of a foreshortened future, as in not expecting to have a long life, marriage, or a career.

C. Symptoms of increased arousal, as in being wounded up or tense, evidenced by:

1. Difficulty falling or staying asleep.
2. Irritability or outbursts of anger.
3. Difficulty concentrating.
4. Hypervigilance, or always being exceptionally watchful of potential danger.
5. Exaggerated startle response, as in jumping or reacting strongly when surprised or frightened.
6. Physical reactions to something that reminds one of the trauma, like sweating or feeling nauseated when seeing a sexual scene in a movie.

Adapted with permission from the *Diagnostic and Statistical Manual of Mental Disorders,* 3rd edition, revised. Copyright © 1987 American Psychiatric Association.

APPENDIX B

GUIDELINES FOR RESPONDING TO DISCLOSURES OF ABUSE

1. Always make your first response sympathetic to the survivor's feelings: "That must have felt awful," or "I'm sorry that happened to you."
2. It is okay to ask, "What do you need from me?" when you do not know what to do or say.
3. Stick with the topic of abuse until the person gives a clear indication that he or she wants to stop talking. If in doubt, ask, "Do you want to stop talking now?"
4. Share your outrage, compassion, and concern with appropriate comments.

5. At the end, you may want to ask the survivor how he or she is feeling now.

6. You may have a delayed reaction to hearing this story, so be sure to notice and meet your emotional needs in the next week or two.

7. Do not request further information without first responding compassionately to the disclosure. Especially avoid asking, "How old were you?" or "How much younger were you than the abuser?"

8. Do not say anything positive or understanding about the perpetrator.

9. Do not ask, "Are you sure?"

10. Do not change the subject. Do not take this opportunity to disclose or speculate on your own abuse issues.

11. Do not get into your own feelings at the expense of the survivor. Keep the focus of attention on the survivor.

12. Do not hug or approach the person physically. If you feel it may be appropriate to hug or pat the person, ask permission first. Remember that the survivor may not be able to say no even if he or she does not want to be touched.

BIBLIOGRAPHY

BASS, ELLEN, and DAVIS, LAURA, *The Courage to Heal*. New York: Harper and Row, 1988.

BEAR, E., and DIMOCK, P., *Adults Molested as Children: A Survivor's Manual for Women and Men*. Orwell: First Society Press, 1988.

BLUME, E. SUE, *Secret Survivors: Uncovering Incest and Its Aftereffects in Women*. New York: John Wiley and Sons, 1990.

BRAUN, B., *Treatment of Multiple Personality Disorder*. Washington, DC.: American Psychiatric Press, Inc., 1986.

BRIERE, JOHN, *Therapy for Adults Molested as Children: Beyond Survival*. New York: Springer Press, 1989.

COURTOIS, CHRISTINE, *Healing the Incest Wound: Adult Survivors in Therapy*. New York: W. W. Norton, 1988.

FINKELHOR, DAVID, *Child Sexual Abuse: New Theory and Research*. New York: Free Press, 1984.

FREDRICKSON, RENEE, *Putting the Pieces Together: Tapes on Recovery*.St. Paul: Fredrickson and Associates, P.A., 1990.

GIL, ELIANA, *United We Stand: A Book for People with Multiple Personalities*. Walnut Creek: Launch Press, 1990.

HOLLINGSWORTH, J., *Unspeakable Acts*. New York: Congden and Weed, 1986.

JACKSON, SHARON, *The Adult Survivor of Ritual Abuse: A Personal Perspective*. Rialto: Motivation Unlimited, 1988.

KLUFT, RICHARD, *Incest-Related Syndromes of Adult Psychopathology*, edited by Richard Kluft. Washington, DC.: American Psychiatric Press, 1990.

LISON, KAREN, AND POSTON, CAROL, *Reclaiming Our Lives*. Boston: Little, Brown and Co., 1989.

MAHRER, A. R., *Dream Work in Psychotherapy and Self-Change*. New York: W. W. Norton and Company, 1989.

MILLER, ALICE, *Banished Knowledge: Facing Childhood Injuries*. New York: Doubleday, 1990.

PETTINATI, HELEN M., *Hypnosis and Memory*, edited by Helen Pettinati. New York: Guilford Press, 1988.

PUTNAM, FRANK W., The study of multiple personality disorder: General strategies and practical considerations. Thorofare: *Psychiatric Annals*, 14:1, January 1984.

WALSH, B. W., and ROSEN, P. M., *Self-Mutilation: Theory, Research, and Treatment*. New York: Guilford Press, 1988.

WHITMONT, E. C., and PERERA, S. B., *Dreams: A Portal to the Source*. New York: Routledge, 1989.

WILSON, JOHN, *Trauma, Transformation, and Healing: An Integrative Approach to Theory, Research, and Post-Traumatic Therapy*. New York: Brunner Mazel, 1989.

WOLF, MARION, and MOSNAUM, ARON, *Post-Traumatic Stress Disorder: Etiology, Phenomenology, and Treatment*. Washington, DC.: American Psychiatric Press, 1990.

INDEX

236 INDEX

Reactions, observation of, 109
Reality
  balanced, appropriate sense of,
    160
  distrust of, 62
  emerging, 21
  family's, challenging, 24
  vs. unreality, 161
Recall memory, 88–89
  See also Memory retrieval
  defined, 88
Recognition signals, 88
Recovery
  See also Healing
  guiding your own, 16–19
Refocusing, 61
Relationships
  difficulties with, 29
  failed, 30
Reminder factor, 42
Remorse, 78
Repressed memories. *See*
  Memory repression
Repressed memory syndrome,
    40–47, 167
  four categories of, 41–47
Rescue
  as choice for protection from
    further abuse, 64
  fantasies, 116
  longing for, 156
Resistance, in imagistic memory
    work, 115–16
Resolution
  in body work, defined, 147
  stage in healing process, 218–
    220
Rewards, of retrieving repressed
    memories, 30
Risk taking, 24–28
Ritual abuse, 113, 154, 164–65
  disclosure about, 199
  survivors, and nightmares,
    126
Role play, 205
Role reversal, 80

Sadistic abuse, 113
Sadness, 93
  symbolic dreams and feelings
    of, 124

Secrecy, 23
Security, feelings of, to face
    abuse, 38
Sedation, with drugs and
    alcohol, 62–63, 67
Selective focus of attention, 150
Self-abusive behavior, as
    symptom of emerging
    memories, 184
Self-blame, 30
Self-centeredness, 78
Self-defeating behaviors, 21, 30
Self-destructive behavior, 29
  See also Injury(ies), self-
    inflicted
  devising protection plan for,
    117
Self-discipline, 113
Self-esteem, 31
  building, 220
Self-hate, 29
Self-hypnosis, 62
  masquerading as disbelief,
    161
Self-hypnotic suggestions, 56
  repetition of, to forget, 66
Sensitivity, 81
Sequencing, in imagistic memory
    work, 111–14
Sex
  of choice, 78
  problems with, 42
Sexism, 78
Sexual abuse, 13–16
  dissociated image of, 60
  dreams, 127
  forgotten, 52–66
  masturbation as sign of, in
    young children, 180–81
  oral, 43
  pain of, forgetting, 39
  reliving scene of, 45
  reminders of, 42–43
  and repressed memories, 23
Sexual dreams, and sexual abuse
    dreams, 127–28
Sexual fantasizing, 78
Sexuality checklist, 48
Shame, 23, 29, 81, 93
  as part of healing process, 217
  sexual, 29